Crafting Cinematic Magic

Unlock the Secrets of Successful Filmmaking

Echo Johnson

The presentation of the information is without contract or any type of guarantee assurance. The trademarks that are used are without any consent, and the publication of the trademark is without permission or backing by the trademark owner. All trademarks and brands within this book are for clarifying purposes only and are the owned by the owners themselves, not affiliated with this document.

Table of Contents

Chapter 1

Introduction to Filmmaking

The Evolution of Cinema

Cinema, an art form that has captivated audiences for over a century, has undergone a remarkable transformation since its inception. The evolution of cinema reflects not only technological advancements but also shifts in cultural and social paradigms. The journey from silent films to the digital age is a testament to the relentless pursuit of innovation by artists and technologists alike.

In the late 19th century, the advent of motion picture cameras marked the birth of cinema. Pioneers like Thomas Edison and the Lumière brothers laid the groundwork for what would become one of the most influential forms of entertainment. Their early experiments with capturing and projecting moving images captivated audiences, who were mesmerized by the novelty of seeing life replicated on screen. The first public screening by the Lumière brothers in 1895 is often heralded as the official birth of cinema. The films were short, simple, and silent, yet they had an undeniable charm that sparked the imagination of viewers.

As cinema began to take hold, it quickly became apparent that this new medium had the potential to do more than just entertain. Filmmakers started experimenting with narrative storytelling, giving rise to the feature film. In the early 20th century, directors like Georges Méliès pushed the boundaries of visual storytelling with films like "A Trip to the Moon," which utilized innovative special effects to create fantastical worlds. This era of cinema was characterized by creativity and experimentation, as filmmakers sought to explore the possibilities of this new art form.

The silent film era reached its zenith in the 1920s, with stars like Charlie Chaplin and Buster Keaton becoming household names. These films relied heavily on physical comedy and visual storytelling, as dialogue was conveyed through intertitles. Despite the absence of sound, silent films were able to evoke a wide range of emotions and communicate complex narratives. Directors like D.W. Griffith further advanced cinematic techniques, introducing innovations such as cross-cutting and close-ups to heighten dramatic tension.

The introduction of synchronized sound in the late 1920s marked a turning point in the evolution of cinema. The release of "The Jazz Singer" in 1927, the first feature-length film with synchronized dialogue, signaled the end of the silent film era and the beginning of the "talkies." This technological breakthrough brought new challenges and opportunities for filmmakers, as they had to adapt to the demands of recording sound while maintaining the visual appeal of their films. The addition of sound also opened up new avenues for storytelling, allowing for more nuanced performances and complex narratives.

The 1930s and 1940s are often referred to as the Golden Age of Hollywood, a period characterized by the studio system and the production of numerous iconic films. During this time, studios like MGM, Warner Bros., and Paramount dominated the industry, producing a steady stream of films that captivated audiences worldwide. The star system flourished, with actors like Humphrey Bogart, Katharine Hepburn, and Clark Gable becoming international icons. Genres such as film noir, musicals, and screwball comedies emerged, each offering unique storytelling conventions and stylistic flourishes.

World War II and its aftermath had a profound impact on cinema, as filmmakers grappled with the realities of a changing world. The post-war era saw the rise of neorealism in Italy, with directors like Roberto Rossellini and Vittorio De Sica using cinema as a tool to depict the harsh realities of life in a war-torn country. These films were characterized by their use of non-professional actors, on-location shooting, and a focus on everyday struggles, offering a stark contrast to the glossy productions of Hollywood.

The 1950s and 1960s brought about significant changes in the film industry, as television emerged as a powerful competitor to cinema. To lure audiences back to theaters, filmmakers experimented with new technologies such as widescreen formats, 3D, and Technicolor. This period also saw the emergence of auteur directors, who sought to assert their artistic vision and push the boundaries of storytelling. Filmmakers like Alfred Hitchcock, Federico Fellini, and Ingmar Bergman crafted films that challenged conventional narrative structures and explored complex themes.

The late 20th century witnessed the rise of blockbuster cinema, driven by advances in special effects and the increasing importance of global box office revenue. Directors like Steven Spielberg and George Lucas revolutionized the industry with films like "Jaws" and "Star Wars," which combined cutting-edge technology with compelling narratives to create immersive cinematic experiences. The blockbuster era was characterized by high production values, extensive marketing campaigns, and a focus on spectacle.

As the 21st century unfolded, digital technology began to reshape the landscape of cinema. The transition from celluloid to digital filmmaking offered new possibilities for filmmakers, allowing for greater flexibility in production and post-production processes. Digital distribution platforms like Netflix and Amazon Prime have also transformed the way audiences consume films, providing access to a vast array of content at the click of a button. This shift has democratized the film industry, enabling independent filmmakers to reach global audiences without the backing of major studios.

In recent years, cinema has continued to evolve in response to cultural and technological shifts. The rise of virtual reality and augmented reality has opened up new avenues for immersive storytelling, while advancements in artificial intelligence and machine learning promise to revolutionize the way films are created and consumed. As filmmakers continue to explore these new technologies, the boundaries of what is possible in cinema are constantly being redefined.

Understanding Film Genres

Film genres are the lifeblood of cinema, providing audiences with a framework to understand and categorize the vast array of stories told on the silver screen. Each genre comes with its own set of conventions, themes, and stylistic elements that guide filmmakers and inform viewers about what to expect. Understanding these genres is crucial not only for filmmakers seeking to craft compelling stories but also for audiences eager to explore the diverse narratives that cinema has to offer.

Genres serve as a shorthand for audiences, offering clues about the type of experience they can anticipate. A romantic comedy promises laughter and love, while a horror film delivers thrills and chills. Filmmakers often play with these expectations, subverting genre conventions to surprise and engage viewers. This interplay between expectation and innovation is at the heart of what makes genres so fascinating.

The action genre is one of the most popular and enduring in cinema, characterized by high-energy sequences, physical stunts, and a fast-paced narrative. These films often revolve around a hero or group of heroes who face overwhelming odds, engaging in battles and confrontations that test their strength and resolve. The action genre is known for its spectacle, with filmmakers utilizing cutting-edge technology and choreography to create thrilling set pieces that leave audiences on the edge of their seats. From classic martial arts films to modern superhero blockbusters, action films continue to captivate audiences with their adrenaline-pumping excitement.

Drama, on the other hand, focuses on character development and emotional depth, exploring complex themes and human experiences. These films often delve into the intricacies of relationships, personal struggles, and moral dilemmas, offering viewers a window into the lives of the characters. Drama films are known for their strong performances and thought-provoking narratives, which encourage audiences to reflect on their own experiences and the world around them. Whether depicting historical events or intimate personal stories, dramas have the power to move and inspire.

Horror films tap into our deepest fears, using suspense, tension, and shock to elicit a visceral response from the audience. The genre is defined by its ability to evoke fear and anxiety, often through supernatural or psychological elements. Horror films explore themes of the unknown, the monstrous, and the terrifying, pushing the boundaries of what is considered acceptable or safe. Filmmakers use a variety of techniques, such as jump scares, eerie soundscapes, and unsettling imagery, to create an atmosphere of dread that lingers long after the credits roll.

Comedy, with its focus on humor and entertainment, provides a welcome escape from the stresses of everyday life. This genre is characterized by its ability to make audiences laugh, often through exaggerated situations, witty dialogue, and physical comedy. Comedies come in many forms, from slapstick and satire to romantic and dark humor, each offering a unique approach to eliciting laughter. While the primary goal is to entertain, many comedies also offer insightful commentary on society, relationships, and human nature, using humor as a tool to illuminate deeper truths.

Science fiction transports audiences to worlds beyond our own, exploring futuristic concepts and speculative ideas. This genre often incorporates elements of technology, space exploration, and the unknown, challenging viewers to consider the possibilities of what lies ahead. Science fiction films are known for their imaginative storytelling and visual effects, which bring to life otherworldly landscapes and advanced technologies. These films often grapple with themes of identity, humanity, and the consequences of scientific advancement, offering both entertainment and introspection.

Fantasy, much like science fiction, creates imaginative worlds filled with magic, mythical creatures, and epic quests. This genre invites audiences to escape into realms where the impossible becomes possible, where heroes embark on journeys to defeat evil and restore balance. Fantasy films are characterized by their rich world-building, enchanting visuals, and timeless themes of good versus evil. Whether drawing inspiration from ancient myths or creating entirely new universes, fantasy films capture the wonder and magic of storytelling.

Thrillers keep audiences on the edge of their seats, weaving narratives filled with suspense, tension, and unexpected twists. This genre often involves crime, espionage, or psychological intrigue, with characters facing high-stakes situations that demand quick thinking and resourcefulness. Thrillers are known for their gripping plots and intense pacing, which keep viewers guessing until the very end. Filmmakers use a variety of techniques, such as clever misdirection, atmospheric music, and tight editing, to maintain a sense of urgency and excitement.

Romance explores themes of love and relationships, capturing the complexities of human connection. This genre often focuses on the emotional journey of characters as they navigate the joys and challenges of falling in love. Romance films can take many forms, from lighthearted rom-coms to sweeping epics, each offering a unique perspective on matters of the heart. These films resonate with audiences by reflecting universal experiences of love, longing, and the search for companionship.

Documentaries, although not a fictional genre, play a crucial role in cinema by presenting real-life stories and events. This genre seeks to inform, educate, and inspire, offering audiences a glimpse into the world around them. Documentaries cover a wide range of topics, from social issues and historical events to personal stories and natural wonders. Filmmakers use various techniques, such as interviews, archival footage, and on-location shooting, to create compelling narratives that engage and enlighten viewers.

The animation genre encompasses a diverse array of styles and techniques, from hand-drawn and stop-motion to computer-generated imagery. Animation allows filmmakers to create worlds and characters limited only by their imagination, offering unique storytelling possibilities. This genre is not confined to children's entertainment; animated films can explore complex themes and appeal to audiences of all ages. The visual artistry and creativity of animation continue to push the boundaries of what is possible in cinema.

Genres are not static; they evolve over time, influenced by cultural shifts, technological advances, and changing audience preferences. Filmmakers often blend elements from multiple genres, creating hybrid films that defy easy classification. This dynamic interplay between genres keeps cinema fresh and exciting, offering endless possibilities for storytelling.

Understanding film genres is an essential skill for both filmmakers and audiences. For filmmakers, it provides a framework for crafting stories that resonate with viewers while allowing for creative experimentation. For audiences, it offers a guide to navigating the diverse landscape of cinema, helping them discover films that align with their tastes and interests.

The Role of a Filmmaker

In the captivating world of cinema, the filmmaker stands as a visionary, orchestrating the myriad elements that bring a story to life on the screen. A filmmaker's role transcends simply directing actors or setting up shots; it involves a profound understanding of storytelling, creativity, and collaboration. The filmmaker is the architect of the cinematic experience, guiding the viewer through a journey of emotions, ideas, and visual splendor.

At the heart of a filmmaker's responsibility is storytelling. Crafting a compelling narrative requires an innate ability to weave together plot, character, and theme into a cohesive whole. The filmmaker must possess an acute sense of timing and pacing, knowing when to build tension, when to provide relief, and how to sustain an audience's engagement throughout the film. This demands a keen understanding of the screenplay as a blueprint for the film's visual and emotional journey.

Collaboration is another cornerstone of the filmmaker's role. Cinema is inherently a collaborative medium, requiring the talents and skills of a diverse team to bring a film to fruition. The filmmaker acts as a conductor, harmonizing the contributions of writers, actors, cinematographers, editors, set designers, and sound engineers. Effective communication is essential, as the filmmaker must articulate their vision clearly and inspire the team to work towards a common goal. This collaboration extends to the relationship with producers, who provide the resources and support necessary to realize the filmmaker's vision.

A filmmaker must also be adept at managing the practical aspects of production. This includes working within budgetary constraints, scheduling shoots, and navigating the logistical challenges that arise during filming. Balancing creativity with practicality is a skill that filmmakers must master, ensuring that their artistic vision is achieved without compromising the project's feasibility. This often involves making difficult decisions, such as cutting scenes or revising the script, to stay on track and within budget.

Visual storytelling is a crucial aspect of filmmaking, and the filmmaker must possess a strong visual sensibility to translate the script into compelling imagery. This entails making choices about camera angles, lighting, composition, and movement to convey the narrative's mood and tone. The filmmaker collaborates closely with the cinematographer to develop a visual style that enhances the story and engages the audience. The use of color, contrast, and framing all contribute to the film's visual identity, creating a cinematic language that communicates on a subconscious level.

The filmmaker's role extends beyond the set, as they are also deeply involved in the post-production process. This phase includes editing, sound design, and visual effects, where the film is shaped and refined into its final form. The filmmaker collaborates with editors to determine the film's rhythm and flow, making decisions about which scenes to include and how to transition between them. Sound design and music play a vital role in augmenting the emotional impact of the film, and the filmmaker works with composers and sound engineers to create an auditory experience that complements the visual elements.

A crucial aspect of a filmmaker's role is to infuse the film with a distinct voice and perspective. This often involves exploring themes and ideas that resonate with the filmmaker, allowing their unique vision to shine through. Whether addressing social issues, personal experiences, or universal truths, the filmmaker has the power to provoke thought and spark conversation. This artistic expression is what sets great filmmakers apart, as they use cinema as a medium to reflect, critique, and celebrate the human condition.

Adaptability is another trait that filmmakers must cultivate. The unpredictable nature of filmmaking means that challenges and setbacks are inevitable, from weather disruptions to technical malfunctions. A successful filmmaker remains flexible and resourceful, finding creative solutions to overcome obstacles without compromising the film's integrity. This adaptability also extends to working with actors, as the filmmaker must create an environment that encourages spontaneity and authenticity in performances.

The filmmaker's role is not static; it evolves with each project and adapts to the ever-changing landscape of the film industry. Technological advancements have opened up new possibilities for storytelling, from digital cinematography to virtual reality. Filmmakers must stay informed about these developments and be willing to experiment with new tools and techniques to enhance their craft. This willingness to innovate is what keeps cinema vibrant and relevant, ensuring that filmmakers can continue to push the boundaries of what is possible on screen.

Essential Filmmaking Terminology

Understanding the language of filmmaking is crucial for anyone aspiring to work in the industry. This specialized vocabulary allows filmmakers, crew members, and actors to communicate effectively on set and in pre- and post-production. Familiarity with essential filmmaking terminology not only aids in collaboration but also empowers you to navigate the world of cinema with confidence and clarity.

A fundamental term that you'll frequently encounter is "frame." In the context of filmmaking, a frame refers to a single image within a sequence of images that make up a film. The concept of framing also pertains to how subjects are composed within the boundaries of the screen. Filmmakers carefully consider framing to convey meaning, focus the viewer's attention, and create visual interest. The rule of thirds, for instance, is a common framing technique that divides the frame into nine equal parts to help balance composition.

"Shot" is another term integral to filmmaking, referring to a continuous recording of a scene or part of a scene. Shots vary in length and type, from the close-up, which provides an intimate view of a subject, to the wide shot, offering a broad perspective of the environment. The choice of shot type serves as a storytelling tool, allowing filmmakers to highlight specific emotions, actions, or details. A "long take" or "oner" is a shot that lasts for an extended period without cuts, often used to create tension or immerse the audience in the moment.

The "storyboard" is an essential pre-production tool that visually represents the sequence of shots planned for a film. These drawings or illustrations outline the composition, camera angles, and movement for each scene, serving as a blueprint for the visual narrative. Storyboards help filmmakers plan the logistics of shooting and communicate their vision to the crew. By providing a visual reference, storyboards ensure that everyone involved in the production is aligned with the director's creative intent.

The term "blocking" refers to the precise staging of actors and camera movements within a scene. Blocking is meticulously planned during rehearsals to ensure that actors move naturally and that the camera captures their performances effectively. Good blocking enhances storytelling by guiding the audience's focus and emphasizing key moments. It also helps maintain continuity and coherence across different shots.

"Diegetic" and "non-diegetic" are terms used to describe sound in film. Diegetic sound originates from sources within the film's world, such as dialogue, footsteps, or a radio playing in a scene. Non-diegetic sound, on the other hand, encompasses elements like background music or a narrator's voice, which are not part of the film's environment. Understanding the distinction between these types of sound helps filmmakers create an auditory landscape that complements the visual narrative and enhances the audience's experience.

"Montage" is a technique that involves editing together a series of short shots to condense time, space, or information. Often used to convey the passage of time or to illustrate a character's development, montages rely on the juxtaposition of images to create meaning. The use of montage can evoke emotion, provide exposition, or generate excitement, making it a powerful tool in a filmmaker's arsenal.

The "continuity" system is a set of editing conventions that maintain a coherent and consistent narrative flow in film. This system ensures that time, space, and action remain logically connected, allowing audiences to follow the story without confusion. Techniques such as match cuts, eye-line matches, and the 180-degree rule are employed to preserve continuity across shots and scenes. Filmmakers must pay close attention to continuity to prevent jarring transitions that might disrupt the viewer's immersion in the story.

"Depth of field" is a term related to cinematography, referring to the range within a shot where objects appear in sharp focus. A shallow depth of field isolates the subject from the background, drawing attention to specific details or emotions. Conversely, a deep depth of field keeps multiple elements in focus, providing context and richness to the scene. Cinematographers manipulate depth of field through aperture settings, lens choice, and camera distance to achieve the desired visual effect.

The "mise-en-scène" encompasses all the visual elements within a frame, including setting, lighting, costume, and actor performance. It is a French term meaning "placing on stage" and reflects the overall aesthetic and visual style of a film. Filmmakers use mise-en-scène to convey tone, mood, and thematic elements, creating a cohesive and immersive world for the audience. Attention to mise-en-scène allows filmmakers to craft a visual language that complements the narrative and enhances storytelling.

"Cross-cutting," also known as parallel editing, is an editing technique that interweaves two or more separate actions occurring simultaneously. This technique creates suspense, builds tension, or draws connections between different plotlines. By cutting back and forth between scenes, filmmakers can highlight thematic or narrative parallels, enhancing the complexity and depth of the story.

"ADR" stands for Automated Dialogue Replacement, a post-production process where actors re-record their dialogue to improve audio quality or reflect changes in the script. This technique is used when original on-set recordings are compromised by background noise or technical issues. ADR sessions require actors to match their vocal delivery to the on-screen performance, ensuring seamless integration into the final film.

The "clapperboard" is a tool used during production to synchronize picture and sound. It consists of a slate with pertinent information such as scene number, take number, and production title, along with a hinged clapstick. The clapperboard is snapped shut at the beginning of a take, creating a visual and auditory reference point for editors to align the footage and audio tracks during the editing process.

"Foley" is the art of creating sound effects in post-production to enhance the auditory experience of a film. Named after sound artist Jack Foley, this process involves recording everyday sounds like footsteps, rustling clothes, or clinking glassware to match the on-screen action. Foley artists use a variety of props and techniques to produce realistic and immersive soundscapes, elevating the overall quality of the film.

Current Trends in the Film Industry

The film industry is a dynamic entity, constantly evolving in response to technological advances, cultural shifts, and audience preferences. In recent years, several trends have emerged that are reshaping the landscape of cinema and influencing how films are made, distributed, and consumed. Understanding these trends is essential for filmmakers and industry professionals looking to navigate the ever-changing world of film.

One of the most significant shifts in the film industry is the rise of streaming platforms. Services like Netflix, Amazon Prime, and Disney+ have transformed the way audiences access and consume content, challenging traditional theatrical distribution models. These platforms offer a vast array of films and series available on-demand, allowing viewers to watch content at their convenience. As a result, filmmakers have new opportunities to reach global audiences without the need for traditional theatrical releases. This shift has also led to increased investment in original content, with streaming giants producing high-quality films and series that rival those of major studios.

The popularity of streaming platforms has also accelerated the trend of binge-watching, where viewers consume multiple episodes or films in a single sitting. This behavior has influenced how filmmakers structure their narratives, with a focus on creating engaging, serialized content that keeps audiences coming back for more. Filmmakers are experimenting with episodic storytelling and cliffhangers to capture and retain viewer attention, blurring the lines between film and television.

Diversity and representation have become central themes in the film industry, as audiences demand more inclusive and authentic stories. Filmmakers and studios are increasingly recognizing the importance of reflecting the diverse world we live in, both in front of and behind the camera. This trend has led to a proliferation of films featuring underrepresented voices, exploring themes of identity, culture, and social justice. The push for diversity extends beyond casting, with efforts to promote inclusivity in all aspects of production, from writers and directors to crew members and executives.

The rise of global cinema is another trend shaping the industry. Audiences worldwide are showing an increasing appetite for films that offer unique cultural perspectives and stories. This has opened the door for filmmakers from different regions to showcase their work on an international stage. The success of films like "Parasite" and "Roma" highlights the growing influence of non-English language cinema and the potential for cross-cultural storytelling to captivate audiences around the globe. Filmmakers are leveraging this trend by collaborating with international talent and exploring universal themes that resonate across borders.

Technological advancements continue to drive innovation in filmmaking, with new tools and techniques enhancing the creative process. Virtual reality (VR) and augmented reality (AR) are opening up new possibilities for immersive storytelling, allowing audiences to interact with and experience narratives in unprecedented ways. While still in the early stages of development, these technologies are poised to revolutionize the way filmmakers engage audiences, offering a more interactive and participatory experience.

The use of digital technology and visual effects has become a staple of modern filmmaking, enabling filmmakers to create stunning visuals and complex worlds that were once impossible to achieve. Advances in computer-generated imagery (CGI) have allowed for more realistic and seamless integration of digital elements with live-action footage. This has expanded the creative potential for filmmakers, enabling them to push the boundaries of storytelling and bring fantastical visions to life.

Sustainability and environmental responsibility have emerged as important considerations in the film industry. As awareness of climate change and environmental impact grows, filmmakers and studios are taking steps to reduce their carbon footprint and promote sustainable practices. This includes initiatives such as green production methods, reducing waste on set, and using energy-efficient equipment. The industry is also exploring ways to incorporate themes of sustainability into storytelling, raising awareness and inspiring audiences to take action.

The rise of independent filmmaking is another trend that has gained momentum in recent years. With the democratization of filmmaking technology and the accessibility of digital distribution platforms, independent filmmakers have more opportunities than ever to create and share their work. This has led to a flourishing of creative expression, with indie films exploring unconventional narratives and pushing the boundaries of traditional storytelling. Crowdfunding and social media have also played a role in supporting independent projects, allowing filmmakers to connect directly with audiences and build a community around their work.

Another trend to watch is the increasing emphasis on experiential cinema. As audiences seek more immersive and engaging experiences, filmmakers are exploring new ways to enhance the theatrical experience. This includes innovations such as 4D cinema, which incorporates sensory effects like motion, scent, and temperature, as well as interactive screenings and live performances. These experiences offer a unique way for audiences to engage with films, creating memorable events that go beyond traditional viewing.

The film industry is also witnessing a growing interest in nostalgia and reboots. Audiences are drawn to familiar stories and characters, leading to a resurgence of classic franchises and the reimagining of beloved films. This trend reflects a desire for comfort and familiarity in uncertain times, as well as the enduring appeal of iconic narratives. Filmmakers are tapping into this nostalgia by revisiting and updating classic stories, offering fresh perspectives while honoring the originals.

In the midst of these trends, the role of the filmmaker remains as vital as ever. Filmmakers are tasked with navigating this rapidly changing landscape, harnessing new technologies, and responding to audience demands while staying true to their creative vision. As the industry continues to evolve, filmmakers will play a crucial role in shaping the future of cinema, exploring new frontiers and telling stories that resonate with audiences worldwide.

Chapter 2

Developing Your Film Concept

Brainstorming Techniques for Original Ideas

Generating original ideas can be a daunting task, especially in an era saturated with content and creativity. However, the art of brainstorming offers a powerful toolkit for unlocking the imagination and developing unique concepts. Whether you're crafting a screenplay, plotting a novel, or conceptualizing a visual project, effective brainstorming techniques can ignite the spark of originality and lead to groundbreaking ideas.

Begin by creating an environment conducive to creativity. A comfortable, inspiring space can significantly influence your ability to think freely and openly. Consider surrounding yourself with objects, images, or sounds that stimulate your imagination. Some people find that playing instrumental music or having artwork nearby helps foster a creative mindset. The goal is to create a sanctuary where ideas can flow without inhibition or judgment.

One of the most well-known brainstorming techniques is mind mapping. This method allows you to visualize connections between different ideas and concepts. Start with a central idea or theme in the middle of a blank page, then branch out with related thoughts and associations. Use lines, colors, and symbols to create a web of interconnected ideas. This visual representation can help you identify patterns and relationships that may not be immediately apparent. Mind mapping encourages nonlinear thinking, which can lead to unexpected and innovative ideas.

Freewriting is another valuable technique for generating original ideas. Set a timer for a specific duration, such as ten or fifteen minutes, and write continuously without worrying about grammar, spelling, or coherence. The objective is to let your thoughts flow unrestricted, capturing the raw essence of your imagination. Freewriting can bypass your internal censor, allowing subconscious ideas to surface. Once the timer ends, review your writing for any intriguing concepts or themes that may have emerged.

The use of prompts can also stimulate creativity. Prompts can be words, images, or questions that serve as a starting point for exploration. Select a prompt that resonates with you and write or draw whatever comes to mind. This exercise encourages you to think beyond your usual patterns and explore new possibilities. Prompts can be particularly useful when you're feeling stuck or uninspired, as they provide a gentle nudge to begin the creative process.

Collaboration is a powerful tool for brainstorming original ideas. Engaging with others allows you to tap into diverse perspectives and experiences. Organize a brainstorming session with friends, colleagues, or fellow creatives, where everyone contributes ideas and builds upon each other's suggestions. This collaborative approach fosters a sense of community and can lead to innovative solutions that might not arise in isolation. Be open to feedback and embrace the diversity of thought that collaboration brings.

Embracing constraints can paradoxically enhance creativity. Limitations can force you to think outside the box and find novel solutions to challenges. Set specific parameters for your brainstorming session, such as a particular theme, genre, or time period. These constraints can serve as a catalyst for creativity, pushing you to explore ideas you might otherwise overlook. By working within defined boundaries, you may discover unexpected avenues for innovation.

Incorporating sensory experiences into your brainstorming process can also unlock original ideas. Engage your senses by listening to different types of music, experimenting with various textures, or exploring new flavors. Sensory experiences can evoke emotions and memories, sparking inspiration and fueling your imagination. Pay attention to how these experiences influence your thoughts and ideas, and consider how they might be integrated into your creative work.

The technique of reverse thinking involves approaching a problem or concept from an opposite perspective. Challenge yourself to consider the reverse of a known idea or theme. For example, if you're brainstorming a story about love, explore the concept of hate or indifference. This exercise encourages you to break free from conventional thinking and explore new angles. By examining the flip side of an idea, you may uncover fresh insights and opportunities for originality.

Visualization is a powerful mental tool for generating creative ideas. Close your eyes and imagine vivid scenes, characters, or scenarios related to your project. Allow your mind to wander and explore different possibilities without constraint. Visualization can help you clarify your vision and inspire new concepts. Once you've visualized a scene or idea, jot down any details or impressions that stand out. This process can serve as a foundation for further exploration and development.

Experimenting with different media can also spark originality. If you're accustomed to writing, try sketching or painting your ideas. If you're a visual artist, consider expressing your concepts through words or music. Working with different media can offer new perspectives and insights, leading to unexpected breakthroughs. The act of translating ideas across different forms can challenge your creativity and expand your creative repertoire.

Finally, remember that patience and persistence are key to successful brainstorming. Original ideas rarely emerge fully formed; they often require time and refinement. Be patient with yourself and allow your ideas to evolve naturally. Revisit your brainstorming notes regularly and continue to build upon them. Over time, seemingly disparate concepts may coalesce into a cohesive and innovative vision.

Crafting a Compelling Storyline

Crafting a compelling storyline is the cornerstone of any successful narrative, whether in film, literature, or theater. A well-constructed storyline captivates the audience, evokes emotion, and leaves a lasting impression. To create such a narrative, one must understand the key elements that contribute to a compelling story and how to weave them together effectively.

Every story begins with an idea—a spark that ignites the imagination. This idea often revolves around a central theme or message that the storyteller wishes to convey. Identifying this core concept is the first step in crafting a storyline that resonates with the audience. Whether it's a tale of love, redemption, or adventure, the theme serves as the backbone of the narrative, guiding the development of characters and plot.

Characters are the heart of any story. They are the vessels through which the audience experiences the narrative, and their journeys are what drive the plot forward. Creating well-rounded, relatable characters is essential for engaging the audience. These characters should possess distinct personalities, motivations, and flaws that make them believable and human. Consider their background, desires, and fears, and how these elements influence their actions and decisions throughout the story.

The protagonist, or main character, is typically the focal point of the narrative. Their journey often involves overcoming obstacles and personal growth, providing a sense of progression and development. Alongside the protagonist, the antagonist presents conflict and challenges, driving the story's tension and drama. A compelling antagonist is not merely a villain but a complex character with their own motivations and depth.

The structure of a storyline is another critical component. A well-structured narrative provides a framework within which the story unfolds, ensuring a coherent and engaging progression. One of the most common structures is the three-act structure, which divides the story into three parts: setup, confrontation, and resolution. The setup introduces the characters, setting, and central conflict, establishing the stakes and drawing the audience in. The confrontation escalates the conflict, presenting challenges and obstacles that test the protagonist. Finally, the resolution brings the story to a satisfying conclusion, resolving the central conflict and providing closure.

Within this structure, the inciting incident serves as a catalyst that propels the protagonist into the main conflict. This event disrupts the status quo and sets the story in motion, capturing the audience's attention and creating a sense of urgency. The inciting incident should be both surprising and inevitable, aligning with the story's theme and characters.

Pacing is another crucial aspect of storytelling. A well-paced narrative maintains the audience's interest by balancing moments of tension and relief. Too much action without respite can be overwhelming, while prolonged lulls can lead to disengagement. Effective pacing involves varying the rhythm of the story, using techniques such as cliffhangers, twists, and reveals to sustain momentum and keep the audience invested.

Dialogue is a powerful tool for advancing the plot and revealing character. Through dialogue, characters express their thoughts, emotions, and intentions, providing insight into their personalities and relationships. Well-crafted dialogue is natural and authentic, reflecting the character's voice and contributing to the story's atmosphere. Subtext, the unspoken meaning behind the words, adds depth and complexity, inviting the audience to read between the lines and engage more deeply with the narrative.

Setting plays a vital role in shaping the story's atmosphere and context. The environment in which the story unfolds can influence the mood, tone, and themes, serving as more than just a backdrop. A richly detailed setting immerses the audience in the story world, enhancing the narrative's believability and impact. Consider how the setting affects the characters and plot, and use sensory details to bring it to life.

Conflict is the driving force of any compelling storyline. It creates tension, drama, and stakes, propelling the narrative forward and engaging the audience emotionally. Conflict can take many forms, from external challenges and adversaries to internal struggles and moral dilemmas. The resolution of these conflicts provides the story's climax, a pivotal moment that delivers emotional payoff and satisfaction.

A compelling storyline also embraces the element of surprise. Unexpected twists and turns can add excitement and intrigue, challenging the audience's expectations and keeping them engaged. These surprises must be carefully crafted to align with the story's logic and character motivations, ensuring they enhance rather than detract from the narrative.

Themes and symbolism add layers of meaning to a story, enriching the audience's experience and inviting reflection. Themes explore universal truths and concepts, resonating with the audience on a deeper level. Symbolism uses objects, characters, or events to represent abstract ideas, adding depth and nuance to the narrative. By weaving themes and symbolism into the storyline, storytellers can create a more profound and thought-provoking experience.

Emotional resonance is the hallmark of a compelling storyline. A story that evokes genuine emotional responses—whether laughter, tears, or contemplation—leaves a lasting impact on the audience. To achieve this, storytellers must connect with their audience on an emotional level, using relatable characters, authentic emotions, and meaningful themes. By crafting a narrative that speaks to the human experience, storytellers can inspire empathy and reflection.

In crafting a compelling storyline, revision and refinement are essential. The initial draft is just the beginning, a foundation upon which to build and improve. Revisiting and revising the narrative allows storytellers to identify and address weaknesses, enhance strengths, and ensure coherence and consistency. Feedback from trusted peers or mentors can provide valuable insights and perspectives, guiding the revision process and helping to elevate the story to its full potential.

Character Development and Depth

Character development is the lifeblood of storytelling, infusing narratives with authenticity and emotional resonance. Characters serve as the audience's conduit into the world of the story, and their journeys are what captivate and engage viewers or readers. Crafting characters with depth and dimension is essential for creating a compelling narrative that leaves a lasting impact.

The process of character development begins with understanding the core essence of your characters. Delve into their backgrounds, personalities, and motivations to create a foundation upon which to build. Consider their upbringing, cultural influences, and life experiences, as these elements shape who they are and how they interact with the world. A well-developed character possesses a rich inner life, with desires, fears, and conflicts that drive their actions and decisions.

One of the most effective ways to develop characters is to explore their goals and motivations. Every character should have a clear objective that guides their journey throughout the narrative. These goals can be external, such as achieving success or overcoming an obstacle, or internal, such as finding self-acceptance or healing from a past trauma. Understanding what drives your characters allows you to create meaningful arcs that reflect their growth and change over time.

Flaws and vulnerabilities are crucial components of character depth. Perfect characters are often unrelatable and uninteresting, as it is their imperfections that make them human. Consider what weaknesses or insecurities your characters possess and how these aspects influence their actions and relationships. Flaws provide opportunities for conflict and tension, as characters grapple with their limitations and strive for self-improvement.

To create believable characters, it's essential to ensure that their actions and decisions align with their established traits and motivations. Consistency in character behavior enhances credibility and allows the audience to form a deeper connection with the characters. However, this doesn't mean that characters must be predictable—on the contrary, they should possess the capacity for growth and change, evolving in response to the challenges they face.

Relationships with other characters play a significant role in character development. Interactions and dynamics between characters reveal their personalities and contribute to their growth. Consider how characters influence each other, and how their relationships evolve over the course of the narrative. These interactions can serve as catalysts for change, prompting characters to confront their beliefs, values, and emotions.

Dialogue is a powerful tool for revealing character depth. Through conversation, characters express their thoughts, emotions, and intentions, providing insight into their personalities. Authentic dialogue reflects a character's voice, capturing their unique way of speaking and thinking. Subtext, the underlying meaning beneath the words, adds complexity and nuance, allowing audiences to discern motivations and emotions that may not be explicitly stated.

The concept of the character arc is fundamental to character development. An arc represents the transformation or evolution of a character over the course of the story. This journey often involves overcoming obstacles, learning valuable lessons, and experiencing personal growth. A well-crafted character arc provides a satisfying and emotionally resonant narrative, as audiences witness the character's development and change.

Antagonists and secondary characters also benefit from depth and development. While the protagonist may be the focal point, well-rounded supporting characters enrich the narrative and contribute to the story's complexity. Consider the motivations and desires of antagonists, allowing them to be more than mere obstacles for the protagonist. By giving depth to all characters, the narrative becomes more layered and engaging.

Empathy is a key element in character development, as it allows audiences to connect with and understand the characters' experiences. By portraying characters with authenticity and emotional depth, storytellers can evoke empathy and compassion from their audience. This connection enhances the impact of the narrative, as viewers or readers become invested in the characters' journeys and outcomes.

To achieve depth in character development, storytellers must embrace the intricacies of human nature. Characters should embody the full spectrum of emotions and experiences, reflecting the complexity of real life. Consider the challenges, triumphs, and contradictions that define your characters, and use these elements to create narratives that resonate on an emotional level.

Experimentation and exploration are vital in the character development process. Allow yourself the freedom to explore different facets of your characters, considering various possibilities and scenarios. This exploration can lead to unexpected insights and revelations, enriching your characters and enhancing the narrative. Be open to revisiting and refining your characters as the story evolves, ensuring that they remain dynamic and compelling.

The Importance of Theme and Message

Understanding the importance of theme and message is crucial for crafting a narrative that resonates with audiences. These elements provide depth and purpose, guiding the direction of the story and illuminating its underlying truths. As the backbone of any narrative, theme and message offer insight into the human condition, provoking thought and reflection long after the final scene has unfolded.

The theme of a story is its central idea or underlying meaning. It is the thread that weaves the narrative together, offering cohesion and unity. Unlike plot, which concerns the sequence of events, theme delves deeper, exploring universal truths and concepts. Themes can range from love, power, and freedom to more complex ideas like identity, morality, and redemption. Identifying the theme of your story helps to anchor the narrative, providing a lens through which the audience can interpret the characters' actions and the unfolding events.

The message, closely related to the theme, is the specific insight or lesson that the storyteller wishes to convey. While the theme is a broad exploration of a concept, the message is more focused, offering commentary or perspective on the theme. For example, a story with a theme of love might convey a message about the enduring power of love to overcome adversity. The message serves as the story's takeaway, the idea that lingers in the audience's mind and heart.

Crafting a compelling theme and message requires introspection and intention. Consider what you want your audience to ponder or feel by the story's end. Reflect on your own beliefs and experiences, as these can inform the themes and messages you wish to explore. A personal connection to the theme can infuse the narrative with authenticity and passion, making it more relatable and impactful.

Integrating theme and message into a narrative involves subtlety and nuance. Rather than explicitly stating the theme or message, allow them to emerge organically through the characters, plot, and setting. Characters' journeys and transformations often reflect the theme, offering insight into the story's deeper meaning. Their struggles, choices, and growth can illuminate the message, providing a rich and layered narrative experience.

The setting can also play a crucial role in reinforcing the theme and message. The environment in which the story takes place can reflect and amplify the central ideas, contributing to the story's atmosphere and tone. For instance, a dystopian setting might underscore themes of power and control, while a lush, natural landscape could evoke themes of freedom and renewal. Consider how the setting interacts with the characters and plot, and how it can be used to enhance the thematic elements of the story.

Conflict is a powerful vehicle for exploring theme and message. It creates tension and stakes, driving the narrative forward and challenging the characters. Through conflict, characters confront their beliefs, values, and desires, prompting introspection and growth. The resolution of these conflicts often reveals the story's message, offering insight into the theme and providing closure for the audience.

Symbolism can add depth and complexity to the theme and message. Symbols are objects, characters, or events that represent larger ideas, offering a visual or metaphorical representation of the theme. They invite the audience to engage with the narrative on a deeper level, encouraging reflection and interpretation. By carefully incorporating symbols into the story, storytellers can enrich the narrative and enhance the impact of the theme and message.

The emotional resonance of a story is intrinsically linked to its theme and message. A narrative that evokes genuine emotion can leave a lasting impression, resonating with audiences on a personal level. To achieve this, storytellers must connect with the audience's emotions, using relatable characters, authentic experiences, and meaningful themes. By crafting a narrative that speaks to the human experience, storytellers can evoke empathy, compassion, and introspection.

Themes and messages can also serve as a catalyst for social change and discussion. Stories have the power to challenge assumptions, provoke thought, and inspire action. By addressing relevant issues and exploring diverse perspectives, storytellers can contribute to meaningful conversations and encourage audiences to reflect on their beliefs and values. A story with a strong theme and message can spark dialogue and inspire change, leaving a lasting impact on society.

As storytellers, it's essential to remain open to the evolution of theme and message throughout the creative process. While initial ideas may serve as a foundation, the narrative may naturally develop and shift as characters and plotlines unfold. Embrace this evolution, allowing the theme and message to grow organically in response to the story's progression. This flexibility can lead to richer, more authentic narratives that resonate deeply with audiences.

Chapter 3
Scriptwriting Essentials

Understanding Screenplay Structure

Screenplay structure serves as the architectural blueprint for any film or television script, guiding the narrative flow and ensuring clarity and coherence. Understanding this structure is essential for both seasoned writers and novices, as it provides a framework to effectively convey story, character, and theme. Whether you're crafting a gripping thriller, a heartfelt drama, or a light-hearted comedy, a well-structured screenplay enhances the storytelling experience and engages the audience from start to finish.

At the heart of screenplay structure is the three-act model, a time-tested framework that divides the narrative into three distinct parts: the setup, confrontation, and resolution. This model provides a clear progression, guiding the audience through the story while maintaining tension and interest. Each act serves a specific purpose, contributing to the overall arc and ensuring a satisfying narrative journey.

The first act, or setup, introduces the audience to the world of the story. It establishes the main characters, setting, and central conflict, providing the foundation upon which the narrative will build. The opening scenes are crucial for capturing the audience's attention and drawing them into the story. This act typically includes the inciting incident, a pivotal event that disrupts the status quo and propels the protagonist into the main conflict. The inciting incident raises the stakes and sets the narrative in motion, creating a sense of urgency and anticipation.

As the story transitions into the second act, or confrontation, the narrative deepens and expands. This act comprises the bulk of the screenplay, presenting the protagonist with a series of challenges and obstacles that test their resolve and character. The confrontation act explores the complexities of the central conflict, delving into the protagonist's relationships, motivations, and growth. Tension and stakes continue to escalate as the protagonist faces setbacks and makes critical decisions. This act often includes a midpoint—a significant turning point that shifts the direction of the narrative and heightens the stakes.

The third act, or resolution, brings the narrative to a satisfying conclusion, resolving the central conflict and providing closure for the audience. This act includes the climax, the story's most intense and decisive moment, where the protagonist confronts the primary antagonist or obstacle. The climax offers emotional payoff and catharsis, as the protagonist's journey reaches its culmination. Following the climax, the denouement wraps up any remaining loose ends, offering a glimpse into the characters' future and the story's lasting impact.

While the three-act structure provides a foundational framework, screenwriters often employ additional techniques to enhance the narrative's complexity and depth. One such technique is the use of subplots—

secondary storylines that run parallel to the main plot. Subplots add dimension to the narrative, exploring different facets of the theme and providing opportunities for character development. They can also intersect with the main plot, influencing the protagonist's journey and contributing to the story's resolution.

Character arcs are another critical component of screenplay structure. A well-crafted character arc demonstrates the protagonist's growth and transformation over the course of the narrative. This journey often involves overcoming internal and external obstacles, leading to self-discovery and change. The character arc parallels the screenplay's structure, with key moments of development occurring at the inciting incident, midpoint, climax, and resolution. By aligning the character arc with the narrative structure, screenwriters can create a cohesive and emotionally resonant story.

Pacing is an essential consideration in screenplay structure, as it influences the story's rhythm and flow. Effective pacing ensures that the narrative maintains momentum, balancing moments of tension and relief to keep the audience engaged. Screenwriters use techniques such as cliffhangers, reveals, and reversals to sustain interest and drive the story forward. By varying the pacing and rhythm, writers can create a dynamic and captivating narrative experience.

Dialogue is a powerful tool within screenplay structure, advancing the plot and revealing character. Through dialogue, characters express their thoughts, emotions, and intentions, providing insight into their personalities and relationships. Well-crafted dialogue is natural and authentic, reflecting the character's voice and contributing to the story's atmosphere. Subtext, the unspoken meaning behind the words, adds depth and complexity, inviting the audience to engage more deeply with the narrative.

Visual storytelling is a defining feature of screenwriting, as the medium of film relies on imagery to convey meaning and emotion. Screenwriters must think visually, considering how scenes will be translated to the screen. Descriptive language, vivid imagery, and dynamic action sequences enhance the narrative's impact, creating a visceral and immersive experience. By focusing on visual elements, screenwriters can convey theme and emotion with subtlety and power.

Understanding screenplay structure also involves recognizing the importance of format and presentation. A screenplay is a technical document, with specific conventions and guidelines that must be followed. Proper formatting ensures clarity and readability, allowing directors, actors, and production teams to interpret the story accurately. Screenwriters must be familiar with industry standards, including scene headings, action descriptions, character names, and dialogue formatting.

In addition to the three-act structure, screenwriters may explore alternative narrative structures to convey unique stories and perspectives. Nonlinear narratives, fractured timelines, and multi-perspective stories offer innovative ways to engage the audience and challenge traditional storytelling conventions. While these structures require careful planning and execution, they can lead to groundbreaking and memorable narratives.

Crafting Dialogue That Resonates

Dialogue is the heartbeat of any narrative, whether in a novel, screenplay, or stage play. It breathes life into characters, advances the plot, and reveals the intricacies of relationships. Crafting dialogue that resonates with audiences is both an art and a science, requiring a keen ear for language and an understanding of character dynamics.

Authenticity is the cornerstone of compelling dialogue. To achieve this, writers must strive to capture the natural rhythms and nuances of speech. Real-world conversations are rarely perfect; they are filled with interruptions, tangents, and quirks. By incorporating these elements into dialogue, writers can create exchanges that feel genuine and relatable. Listening to how people speak in everyday life, paying attention to their vocabulary, cadence, and patterns, can provide valuable insights for crafting believable dialogue.

Each character should possess a distinct voice, reflecting their background, personality, and worldview. This uniqueness is achieved through careful consideration of word choice, sentence structure, and tone. For instance, a character who is highly educated may use formal language and complex sentences, while a more laid-back character might favor colloquialisms and a casual tone. By ensuring each character speaks in a way that is true to their identity, writers can enhance the depth and authenticity of the narrative.

Subtext is a powerful tool in dialogue, adding layers of meaning beneath the surface. In many conversations, what is left unsaid is just as important as what is spoken. Characters may express their true feelings or intentions indirectly, through implication or suggestion. This creates tension and intrigue, inviting audiences to read between the lines and engage more deeply with the story. Mastering the use of subtext allows writers to convey emotions and motivations subtly and effectively.

Conflict and tension are often the driving forces behind engaging dialogue. When characters have differing goals, opinions, or desires, their exchanges become charged with energy and intensity. Conflict can arise from external circumstances or internal struggles, providing opportunities for characters to assert themselves, challenge each other, and reveal their true selves. By crafting dialogue that is dynamic and confrontational, writers can propel the narrative forward and maintain audience interest.

Exposition, while necessary for providing context and information, can be challenging to integrate into dialogue without feeling forced or unnatural. The key is to weave exposition seamlessly into the conversation, allowing characters to reveal necessary details through their natural interactions. This can be achieved by using conflict, humor, or emotion to mask the exposition, ensuring the information is delivered in an engaging and organic manner.

Pacing is another critical element of effective dialogue. The rhythm and tempo of exchanges can greatly influence the overall flow of the narrative. Rapid-fire dialogue can heighten tension and urgency, while slower, more deliberate exchanges can create intimacy and reflection. Varying the pace of dialogue helps maintain audience engagement and mirrors the emotional beats of the story. Writers should consider the emotional state of their characters and the context of the scene when determining the appropriate pacing.

Silence and pauses can be just as impactful as spoken words. Moments of silence allow characters to process information, reflect on their emotions, or build anticipation. Pauses can create a sense of realism, as characters gather their thoughts or hesitate before speaking. By incorporating silence and pauses strategically, writers can add depth and nuance to their dialogue, heightening the emotional impact of the scene.

Humor is a valuable tool in dialogue, offering levity and relief in tense or dramatic narratives. It can reveal character traits, such as wit or sarcasm, and strengthen relationships through shared laughter. However, humor should be used judiciously, ensuring it aligns with the tone of the story and the personalities of the characters. When executed well, humor can make dialogue more memorable and endearing to audiences.

Repetition and callbacks can enhance the resonance of dialogue, creating connections and reinforcing themes. A repeated phrase or motif can serve as a reminder of a character's journey or an underlying message. Callbacks to earlier conversations or events can evoke nostalgia or highlight character growth. By thoughtfully employing repetition and callbacks, writers can create dialogue that resonates on a deeper level.

Editing and refinement are essential steps in crafting impactful dialogue. The first draft is an opportunity to explore ideas and experiment with character voices. Subsequent revisions allow writers to polish the dialogue, ensuring clarity, authenticity, and resonance. Reading dialogue aloud can provide valuable insights into its flow and effectiveness, helping writers identify areas for improvement. Peer feedback can also offer fresh perspectives and suggestions for enhancing dialogue.

Techniques for Visual Storytelling

Visual storytelling is a powerful art form that transcends language and culture, conveying emotions, ideas, and narratives through imagery and symbolism. Whether in film, graphic novels, or other visual media, the ability to tell a story through pictures alone can captivate audiences, evoke deep emotions, and leave a lasting impression. Understanding and mastering techniques for visual storytelling is essential for creators who wish to engage their audience in a meaningful and immersive way.

The foundation of visual storytelling lies in composition, the deliberate arrangement of elements within a frame. Composition guides the viewer's eye and creates a focal point, emphasizing the most critical aspects of the scene. The rule of thirds is a fundamental principle, dividing the frame into a grid with two horizontal and two vertical lines. Placing key elements along these lines or their intersections can create balance and harmony, making the image more aesthetically pleasing and impactful. However, breaking away from this rule can also be effective, leading to dynamic and unexpected compositions that draw attention.

Lighting plays a crucial role in setting the mood and tone of a visual narrative. It can evoke emotion, highlight important details, and create depth and dimension. High-key lighting, characterized by bright and even illumination, often conveys a sense of positivity and openness. In contrast, low-key lighting, with its heavy use of shadows and contrast, can evoke mystery, tension, or drama. The direction, color, and intensity of light all contribute to the story being told, influencing the audience's perception and emotional response.

Color is a powerful storytelling tool, capable of conveying mood, emotion, and symbolism. Different colors can evoke specific feelings or associations; for example, warm colors like red and orange can suggest passion or danger, while cool colors like blue and green might evoke calmness or melancholy. Color palettes can also be used to differentiate settings, signify character traits, or highlight changes in mood or theme. Consistency and intentionality in color choices can enhance the coherence and impact of the visual narrative.

Camera angles and perspectives significantly influence how a story is perceived. A high angle can make a character appear vulnerable or insignificant, while a low angle can convey power or dominance. Point-of-view shots immerse the audience in a character's experience, creating a sense of intimacy and involvement. Wide shots establish context and setting, while close-ups emphasize emotion and detail. By thoughtfully selecting and varying camera angles, creators can guide the audience's perception and emotional engagement.

Movement within a visual narrative adds dynamism and energy, guiding the viewer's attention and enhancing the storytelling. This movement can be literal, such as a character walking through a scene, or more abstract, such as the movement of light or shadow across a surface. The pacing of movement, whether fast and frenetic or slow and deliberate, can influence the narrative's tension and rhythm. By controlling the flow of movement, creators can manipulate the audience's emotional journey and maintain engagement.

Symbolism and metaphor enrich visual storytelling by adding layers of meaning and inviting interpretation. Objects, colors, or actions can symbolize broader concepts or themes, allowing creators to convey complex ideas without explicit explanation. For instance, a broken mirror might symbolize shattered identity or truth, while a recurring motif of water could represent change or renewal. By incorporating symbolism into their visuals, creators can deepen the narrative and encourage audiences to reflect and engage more deeply.

Editing and sequencing are essential in shaping the narrative arc and pacing of a visual story. The order and timing of shots influence the audience's understanding and emotional response. Techniques such as cross-cutting, match cuts, or jump cuts can create connections, contrasts, or surprises, enhancing the narrative's impact. The rhythm of editing, whether fast-paced and energetic or slow and contemplative, can mirror the emotional beats of the story and maintain audience engagement.

Sound, although not a visual element, plays a vital role in complementing and enhancing visual storytelling. Music, sound effects, and dialogue add depth and texture, influencing the mood and atmosphere. A well-chosen soundtrack can evoke specific emotions, while strategic use of silence can heighten tension or focus attention. Synchronizing sound with visuals can create a more immersive and cohesive experience, drawing the audience further into the narrative world.

Character design and development are integral to visual storytelling, as characters are often the audience's primary connection to the narrative. A character's appearance, mannerisms, and expressions convey personality, motivation, and emotion. Consistency in character design, combined with dynamic and expressive animation or acting, can enhance the believability and relatability of characters. By investing in character development, creators can create memorable and impactful narratives that resonate with audiences.

Revising and Polishing Your Script

Revising and polishing a script is an indispensable step in the writing process, transforming a rough draft into a refined and compelling narrative. It demands patience, persistence, and a discerning eye, as the goal is to enhance clarity, coherence, and impact. Through meticulous revision, writers can elevate their work, ensuring it resonates with audiences and fulfills its creative potential.

The revision process begins with a comprehensive review of the script, assessing its overall structure and flow. This involves stepping back from the details and examining the narrative as a whole. Consider whether the story arc is coherent and if the pacing maintains interest and momentum. Reflect on the effectiveness of the three-act structure or any alternative framework used. Determine if the inciting incident, climax, and resolution are clearly defined and impactful, creating a satisfying journey for the audience.

Character development is another critical aspect to address during revision. Evaluate the depth and consistency of each character, ensuring they possess distinct voices, motivations, and growth arcs. Characters should evolve throughout the narrative, facing challenges and making choices that reveal their true selves. Dialogue should reflect their unique personalities, contributing to authenticity and engagement. By refining character portrayal, writers can create more relatable and multidimensional figures that resonate with audiences.

Dialogue often requires significant attention during the revision process. Authenticity and naturalness are key, as dialogue should mimic real speech while advancing the plot and revealing character. Consider whether conversations feel genuine and if subtext is effectively employed. Look for opportunities to trim unnecessary exposition, opting instead to show rather than tell. Ensure that every line serves a purpose, whether it adds tension, humor, or emotional depth. Reading dialogue aloud can help identify awkward phrasing or stilted exchanges.

Thematic clarity is crucial for a polished script, as it provides depth and meaning. Revisit the central themes and messages, ensuring they are woven seamlessly throughout the narrative. Consider whether symbols, motifs, or recurring imagery effectively reinforce the theme. Reflect on whether the script prompts reflection or discussion, leaving a lasting impression on the audience. By enhancing thematic elements, writers can imbue their work with greater significance and resonance.

Consistency is essential in maintaining the believability of the script. Check for continuity errors, such as inconsistencies in character details, setting, or timeline. Ensure that plot developments align logically and that character actions are motivated and credible. Small inconsistencies can disrupt the audience's suspension of disbelief, so attention to detail is paramount. Create a timeline or character profiles if necessary to track details and maintain coherence.

Pacing and rhythm are vital to sustaining audience engagement. Consider the balance between fast-paced and slower, introspective scenes. Evaluate whether transitions between scenes are smooth and if the script maintains momentum. Adjustments to pacing can enhance tension, emotional impact, or comedic timing, depending on the narrative's needs. By varying the rhythm, writers can create a dynamic and captivating experience that holds the audience's attention.

Visual storytelling should not be overlooked during revision. As scripts are intended for visual media, consider how scenes will translate to the screen. Assess descriptions for clarity and vividness, ensuring they effectively convey the intended imagery and mood. Explore opportunities to incorporate visual symbolism, enhancing the narrative's depth and richness. By focusing on the visual aspect, writers can create a more immersive and engaging experience for the audience.

Feedback is an invaluable tool in the revision process, offering fresh perspectives and insights. Share the script with trusted peers, mentors, or writing groups, inviting constructive criticism and suggestions. Consider feedback with an open mind, recognizing that different viewpoints can reveal blind spots or areas for improvement. While not all feedback will align with the writer's vision, it can provide valuable guidance and inspire creative solutions.

Editing for grammar, punctuation, and formatting is the final step in polishing a script. Attention to these details ensures professionalism and readability, making it easier for directors, actors, and production teams to interpret the work. Adhering to industry-standard formatting conventions is crucial, as it demonstrates familiarity with the medium and respect for collaborators. Proofreading multiple times, or enlisting the help of an editor, can catch errors that might otherwise go unnoticed.

Chapter 4
Pre-Production Planning

Assembling Your Creative Team

Bringing a story to life is rarely a solo endeavor. Behind every successful script is a talented and dedicated creative team working in harmony to transform words on a page into a vivid, compelling experience. Assembling this team is a crucial step in the journey from script to screen, requiring thoughtful consideration of skills, vision, and collaboration.

The director is often the first and most critical member of the creative team. As the visionary leader, the director interprets the script and shapes the artistic and dramatic aspects of the film. This role demands a blend of creativity, leadership, and communication skills, as the director must guide the entire team while maintaining a cohesive vision. Finding a director who shares your passion and understanding of the story is essential, as their influence will permeate every aspect of production.

A cinematographer, or director of photography, is responsible for capturing the visual essence of the script. This role involves selecting camera angles, lighting, and shot composition to convey the desired mood and atmosphere. A skilled cinematographer collaborates closely with the director to ensure the visual storytelling aligns with the narrative goals. Their technical expertise and artistic sensibility are crucial in bringing the story to life on screen.

The production designer plays an integral role in creating the film's world, crafting sets, and selecting locations that support the narrative. They work closely with the director and cinematographer to ensure the visual style is consistent and cohesive. Attention to detail and creativity are paramount, as the production designer must transform abstract ideas into tangible environments that enhance the story's impact.

Casting directors are tasked with finding the right actors to embody the characters, a process that can make or break a production. They must understand the nuances of each role and identify performers who can bring depth and authenticity to the characters. The casting director collaborates with the director and producers to ensure that the ensemble cast works harmoniously, contributing to the overall success of the narrative.

The costume designer is responsible for the visual storytelling that extends to the characters' attire. Costumes can reveal much about a character's personality, status, and evolution, supporting the narrative without the need for dialogue. A skilled costume designer collaborates with the director and production designer to ensure that the wardrobe aligns with the story's setting and tone.

A sound designer crafts the auditory experience, adding depth and emotion to the visual narrative. This role involves creating soundscapes, selecting music, and crafting sound effects that complement the story. Sound design can significantly enhance the audience's emotional engagement, making it a vital component of the creative team.

The editor is responsible for shaping the final product, assembling the raw footage into a coherent and compelling narrative. This role demands a keen understanding of pacing, rhythm, and storytelling. The editor works closely with the director to ensure that the final cut reflects the intended vision, often making critical decisions that impact the narrative's flow and emotional impact.

Producers are the logistical and financial backbone of the creative team, overseeing the project's development from start to finish. They manage budgets, schedules, and resources, ensuring that the production runs smoothly and efficiently. A skilled producer balances creative aspirations with practical considerations, making them an invaluable asset to the team.

Collaboration is the cornerstone of assembling a creative team, as each member brings unique talents and perspectives to the project. Effective communication is essential, as it ensures that everyone remains aligned with the shared vision and goals. Regular meetings, clear directives, and open dialogue can foster a collaborative environment where creativity thrives.

Diversity within the creative team can enrich the storytelling process, bringing fresh perspectives and ideas to the table. Embracing diverse voices and backgrounds can lead to more authentic and relatable narratives, resonating with a broader audience. When assembling your team, consider the value that diverse experiences and viewpoints can bring to the project.

Trust and respect are fundamental to a successful creative team. Each member must feel empowered to contribute their expertise and ideas, knowing that their input is valued and considered. Building trust fosters a positive and productive working environment, where team members feel motivated to give their best effort.

Flexibility and adaptability are also essential qualities for a creative team, as the production process is often unpredictable. Challenges and obstacles are inevitable, requiring the team to think on their feet and find innovative solutions. A team that can adapt to changing circumstances will be better equipped to overcome setbacks and deliver a successful final product.

Budgeting and Financing Your Film

Budgeting and financing are the backbone of any film project, setting the parameters for what can be achieved creatively and logistically. Without a well-structured budget and reliable financing, even the most promising script can falter. Understanding the intricacies of film budgeting and securing the necessary funds are crucial steps in bringing a cinematic vision to life.

Creating a detailed budget starts with a comprehensive breakdown of the film's production requirements. This involves listing all potential expenses, from pre-production through post-production. Begin by identifying the key elements:

cast and crew salaries, equipment rental, location fees, set design, costumes, and special effects. Each category should be meticulously examined to ensure accuracy and completeness. It's essential to account for both major expenses and smaller, often overlooked costs, such as permits, insurance, and catering.

Labor costs typically represent a significant portion of the budget. Negotiating salaries and contracts with cast and crew requires a balance between attracting talented professionals and staying within financial constraints. Consideration should be given to union regulations, which may dictate minimum wages and working conditions. For independent productions, assembling a passionate team willing to work for reduced rates or deferred payment can help manage costs.

Equipment and technology play a vital role in the production process. The choice between renting and purchasing equipment depends on the project's duration and budget. Renting may offer access to high-quality gear without the upfront investment, while purchasing can be cost-effective for longer shoots. Advances in technology have also made certain equipment more affordable, allowing filmmakers to achieve professional results with a tighter budget.

Securing locations that match the script's vision, while staying within budgetary limits, can be challenging. Location scouting is a critical step, requiring negotiation of fees and permits. Filming in certain areas may offer tax incentives or rebates, providing potential savings. Additionally, finding locations that require minimal set dressing or modification can reduce expenses related to art direction and set construction.

Contingency funds are an essential component of any film budget, providing a financial cushion for unforeseen expenses or emergencies. Industry standards suggest setting aside 5-10% of the total budget for contingencies. This reserve can cover unexpected costs such as weather-related delays, equipment malfunctions, or additional shooting days. Having a contingency plan ensures the production remains on track despite potential setbacks.

Once the budget is established, the next step is securing financing. This process often involves a combination of funding sources, including personal investment, private investors, grants, sponsorships, and loans. Each avenue has its own set of challenges and advantages, and a strategic approach can maximize funding opportunities.

Personal investment is often the first step for filmmakers, demonstrating commitment to the project. This can include personal savings or contributions from friends and family. While it may not cover the entire budget, personal investment can serve as leverage when approaching other investors, showcasing belief in the project's potential.

Private investors can provide significant funding, but convincing them to invest requires a compelling pitch and a solid business plan. Potential investors will want to see a clear vision for the project, an understanding of the target audience, and a strategy for distribution and potential returns. Building relationships within the industry and networking at film festivals and events can lead to valuable connections with investors.

Grants and sponsorships are additional sources of funding, often available through film commissions, cultural organizations, or private foundations. These funds may have specific criteria or themes, requiring filmmakers to tailor their projects to align with the grant's objectives. The application process can be competitive and time-consuming, but successful applicants gain not only financial support but also recognition and credibility.

Crowdfunding has emerged as a popular method for financing independent films, leveraging the power of online platforms to reach a global audience. By engaging with potential supporters through social media and offering rewards or incentives, filmmakers can raise funds while building a community around their project. Successful crowdfunding campaigns require careful planning, engaging content, and consistent communication with backers.

Traditional bank loans or film financing companies are another option, though they often require collateral or a track record of successful projects. These loans can provide substantial funding but come with the risk of debt if the film does not achieve financial success. Filmmakers must weigh the potential benefits against the risks and consider the repayment terms carefully.

The distribution strategy is a crucial consideration when planning financing, as it impacts potential revenue streams and investor returns. Understanding the distribution landscape, including theatrical releases, streaming platforms, and international markets, can inform both the budget and financing approach. Collaborating with experienced distributors or sales agents can provide valuable insights and increase the project's marketability.

Throughout the budgeting and financing process, transparency and accountability are paramount. Keeping detailed records and maintaining open communication with investors and stakeholders fosters trust and confidence. Regular updates on the project's progress and financial status can reassure investors and demonstrate responsible management.

Location Scouting and Set Design

The art of location scouting and set design is a critical component of filmmaking, where imagination meets reality to create the world in which a story unfolds. This aspect of production requires a meticulous eye for detail, an understanding of narrative requirements, and the ability to transform ordinary spaces into extraordinary cinematic experiences. Through thoughtful selection and design, filmmakers can enhance the visual storytelling and immerse audiences in the film's universe.

Location scouting begins with a thorough analysis of the script, identifying key scenes and their environmental needs. Each location must serve the story, reflecting the mood, tone, and cultural context of the narrative. The scout's role is to find spaces that not only fulfill these requirements but also offer logistical feasibility, such as accessibility, necessary permits, and budget constraints. A comprehensive understanding of the narrative ensures that the chosen locations enhance the storytelling rather than detract from it.

Once the script's demands are clear, the search for locations commences. This involves exploring diverse environments—urban areas, rural landscapes, historical sites, or even specific architectural styles—that match the script's descriptions. A keen eye for detail is essential, as the scout must envision how a location will appear on camera and assess its potential for transformation. Photographs and videos of potential sites are valuable tools in this process, allowing the creative team to visualize how different settings might complement the narrative.

Collaboration with local authorities and property owners is a crucial part of location scouting. Securing permits and agreements requires clear communication and negotiation skills. Understanding local regulations, potential restrictions, and any community concerns ensures a smooth relationship with those who control access to the desired locations. This aspect of scouting emphasizes the importance of diplomacy and professionalism in navigating the logistical challenges that accompany filming in real-world environments.

Set design comes into play when locations are either unavailable or insufficient to meet the script's needs. This creative process involves constructing environments from scratch to achieve the desired aesthetic and functional requirements. Set designers work closely with directors, production designers, and cinematographers to ensure that the constructed environments align with the film's visual style and narrative goals. The design process begins with conceptual sketches and mood boards, translating abstract ideas into tangible plans.

Material selection is a key consideration in set design, as it impacts both the visual authenticity and practicality of the constructed environment. Designers must choose materials that convey the intended time period, location, and atmosphere, while also considering budget and ease of construction. The use of textures, colors, and patterns plays a significant role in reinforcing the narrative's themes and emotional undertones. Each element must contribute to a cohesive and believable world that draws the audience into the story.

Lighting is an integral part of both location and set design, influencing the mood and tone of each scene. Natural lighting conditions at a location must be considered, as they can affect the scheduling and visual outcome of filming. For sets, designers work with cinematographers to plan artificial lighting setups that enhance the visual storytelling. The interplay between light and shadow can evoke specific emotions, highlight important details, and guide the audience's focus. Mastery of lighting techniques allows filmmakers to manipulate the visual narrative with precision.

The integration of props and set dressing further enhances the authenticity and depth of a location or set. Props are not merely decorative; they serve as extensions of character and plot, providing context and subtext to the narrative. Thoughtful selection and placement of props can reveal character traits, signify thematic elements, and enrich the storytelling. Set dressers meticulously arrange these elements to create lived-in spaces that feel organic and true to the story.

Adaptability is a necessary skill in location scouting and set design. Unforeseen challenges—such as weather conditions, permit delays, or structural limitations—may require creative problem-solving and flexibility. The ability to adapt and find innovative solutions ensures that the production remains on schedule and within budget. This resilience is vital in overcoming obstacles without compromising the artistic vision of the project.

The collaboration between location scouts, set designers, and the broader creative team is essential to the success of the film's visual narrative. Regular communication and feedback loops ensure that all team members are aligned with the project's goals and can contribute their expertise effectively. This collaborative spirit fosters a shared commitment to creating a visually stunning and cohesive film that resonates with audiences.

Scheduling and Shooting Plans

Crafting a film is akin to orchestrating a symphony, where each section must harmoniously align to create a cohesive masterpiece. Scheduling and shooting plans are the sheet music of this symphony, providing structure and ensuring each element of production plays its part at the right moment. These plans are critical in transforming a film from an abstract vision into a tangible reality, demanding meticulous attention to detail, foresight, and adaptability.

The foundation of any successful shoot begins with a well-structured shooting schedule, strategically designed to maximize efficiency and resource use. This schedule is a detailed blueprint, mapping out every scene, location, and day of production. It accounts for the availability of actors, crew, and locations, as well as the logistical considerations that can impact the shoot. A comprehensive shooting schedule minimizes downtime and ensures that the production remains on track and within budget.

Breaking down the script into a shooting schedule requires careful analysis. Each scene is assessed for its logistical demands, including location, time of day, required cast, and special effects or stunts. This breakdown process helps identify potential challenges and resource needs, allowing for informed decision-making. For instance, scenes that occur in the same location or feature the same actors are often grouped together to minimize movement and setup time, streamlining the shooting process.

Prioritizing scenes based on their complexity and importance is a strategic approach that can significantly enhance the efficiency of a shoot. High-impact scenes that require extensive preparation or resources should be scheduled early in the production, while simpler scenes can fill gaps or be used as buffers. This prioritization ensures that crucial moments are captured when energy and focus are at their peak, reducing the risk of compromising on quality due to fatigue or time constraints.

Weather and lighting conditions play a pivotal role in scheduling, particularly for outdoor shoots. Understanding the natural light available at different times of day and anticipating weather patterns is crucial in planning. By scheduling scenes that rely on specific lighting conditions or weather early in the shoot, filmmakers can take advantage of optimal conditions and have time to reshoot if necessary. This foresight minimizes disruptions and maximizes the aesthetic quality of the film.

The shooting schedule must also account for the human element, balancing the demands of the production with the well-being of the cast and crew. Long hours and demanding conditions can lead to fatigue and reduced performance, so it is essential to include regular breaks and reasonable working hours. This consideration not only maintains morale and productivity but also ensures the safety and health of everyone involved.

Creating a flexible schedule is vital to accommodating unforeseen changes or challenges. Contingency days should be built into the plan, allowing for weather delays, equipment malfunctions, or other unexpected events. This flexibility enables the production to adapt to changing circumstances without derailing the entire schedule. A well-prepared team can pivot and adjust plans as needed, maintaining momentum and minimizing disruptions.

Once the schedule is established, a detailed shooting plan outlines the specific actions required to execute each scene. This plan includes camera setups, shot lists, and technical requirements, providing a clear roadmap for the crew. Collaboration between the director, cinematographer, and assistant director is essential in developing a shooting plan that aligns with the creative vision and logistical realities.

The shot list is a crucial component of the shooting plan, detailing every angle and composition needed for each scene. This list ensures that no critical shots are overlooked and helps the team efficiently move from one setup to the next. By organizing shots in a logical sequence, the crew can minimize camera and equipment movement, enhancing the flow and efficiency of the shoot.

Effective communication is the linchpin of successful scheduling and shooting plans. Regular meetings and updates keep all team members informed and aligned with the production's goals. Clear communication channels ensure that any changes or issues are promptly addressed, allowing for swift resolution and minimal disruption. This collaborative environment fosters a sense of unity and shared purpose, motivating everyone to contribute their best effort.

Technology can be a valuable ally in managing scheduling and shooting plans, offering tools and software that streamline the process. Digital platforms allow for real-time updates, accessible to all team members, and provide a centralized hub for scheduling, shot lists, and production notes. By leveraging technology, filmmakers can enhance organization, communication, and efficiency, reducing the administrative burden and focusing on creative execution.

Despite meticulous planning, the unpredictable nature of filmmaking means that challenges are inevitable. Adaptability and problem-solving skills are essential qualities for any production team, enabling them to navigate obstacles and find creative solutions. A positive and resilient mindset can turn setbacks into opportunities for innovation, strengthening the team's cohesion and commitment to the project.

Casting Finding the Right Talent

Casting is the alchemy that transforms a script into a living, breathing narrative. Finding the right talent is not merely about selecting actors who can perform; it's about discovering individuals who can embody characters, bring them to life, and resonate with audiences on an emotional level. The process of casting is both an art and a science, requiring intuition, insight, and a keen understanding of the story's needs.

The journey of casting begins with a thorough understanding of the script and its characters. Each character is a unique entity, with specific traits, arcs, and relationships that drive the story forward. A deep dive into the script allows the casting team to identify the essential qualities each actor must possess. Whether it's the resilience of a protagonist or the complexity of an antagonist, these characteristics form the blueprint for the ideal performer.

A casting director plays a pivotal role in this process, serving as the bridge between the vision of the screenplay and the talent pool. They work closely with the director and producers to define the casting requirements and develop a strategy for finding the right actors. This collaboration ensures that everyone involved shares a unified vision of what each character should be and how they fit into the overall narrative.

The casting director's network of contacts becomes an invaluable resource. Agents, managers, and talent scouts provide access to a diverse array of actors, each bringing their own unique strengths and potential to the project. Open casting calls and auditions widen the net, allowing undiscovered talent the chance to shine. These sessions are a melting pot of potential, where the unexpected can often lead to the most inspired choices.

During auditions, the casting team looks beyond mere technical ability. They seek authenticity, presence, and chemistry. An actor's ability to connect with the material, inhabit the character, and engage with other performers is paramount. Auditions become a space for exploration and experimentation, where actors can interpret the character in ways that might surprise and delight the casting team.

Chemistry reads are an essential part of the casting process, especially for ensemble casts or characters with significant relationships. These sessions allow the team to observe how actors interact and connect with one another. The chemistry between performers can elevate the material, creating dynamics that are palpable and compelling. Finding that synergy is crucial for the believability and emotional impact of the story.

Diversity and representation in casting are increasingly recognized as vital elements of storytelling. Reflecting the multifaceted nature of society enriches the narrative and broadens its appeal. By embracing diverse casting, filmmakers can tell stories that resonate with a wider audience and provide opportunities for underrepresented talent.

This commitment to inclusivity not only enhances the film's authenticity but also contributes positively to the industry as a whole.

The decision-making process in casting can be challenging, as it involves balancing artistic vision with practical considerations. Factors such as an actor's availability, past work, reputation, and audience appeal all play a role. However, the ultimate decision often rests on an ineffable quality—a gut feeling that an actor is the perfect fit for a role. Trusting this instinct, honed by experience and intuition, is key to making inspired casting choices.

Once the cast is assembled, the focus shifts to preparation and rehearsals. This stage is crucial for building rapport and understanding among the cast and crew. Rehearsals provide a safe space for actors to explore their characters, experiment with their performance, and receive feedback. This collaborative environment fosters creativity and growth, allowing the cast to fully embody their roles.

The director's guidance is instrumental during this phase, as they help actors navigate the emotional and psychological terrain of their characters. Through constructive feedback and open dialogue, the director ensures that each performance aligns with the film's vision while allowing room for the actor's personal interpretation. This balance between direction and freedom is essential for achieving authentic and nuanced performances.

As production begins, the cast's ability to adapt and respond to the demands of the shoot is tested. The dynamic nature of filmmaking requires flexibility and resilience, as scenes may be shot out of sequence or adjusted on the fly. A strong rapport among the cast and crew facilitates a supportive and collaborative atmosphere, where challenges are met with creativity and enthusiasm.

Throughout the production, the bond between the cast deepens, often resulting in performances that are layered and emotionally resonant. The chemistry and trust developed during rehearsals translate to the screen, enriching the audience's experience and drawing them into the story. The cast's dedication and passion for their roles become a driving force behind the film's success.

Chapter 5

Directing with Vision

Developing Your Directorial Style

Developing a directorial style is a journey of self-discovery and artistic expression, an exploration of the unique voice that a director brings to the cinematic world. It's an intricate blend of personal vision, storytelling instincts, and technical expertise, all woven together to create a signature approach that distinguishes one's work from others. This chapter delves into the process of cultivating a directorial style, offering insights and strategies for emerging directors to find and refine their cinematic voice.

Every director's style begins with a foundation of influences, both conscious and subconscious. These influences can range from the films and directors that have inspired you, to literature, art, music, and personal experiences that have shaped your worldview. Reflecting on these influences is crucial in understanding the elements that resonate with you and how they might manifest in your own work. Identifying what captivates you about certain films or directors—be it their narrative structure, visual composition, or thematic depth—can provide valuable clues about your preferences and potential style.

The exploration of your own themes and motifs is another vital step in developing a directorial style. What stories are you drawn to tell? What themes repeatedly emerge in your work? These recurring elements often form the backbone of a director's style, providing a thematic continuity that audiences come to recognize and appreciate. Whether it's an exploration of identity, a fascination with human relationships, or a commentary on societal issues, these themes become the lens through which you view and interpret the world.

As you embark on your directorial journey, experimentation is your ally. Embrace opportunities to direct a variety of projects—short films, music videos, commercials, or even theater productions. Each project offers a chance to explore different genres, techniques, and storytelling methods. This hands-on experience is invaluable in discovering what works for you and what doesn't, helping to refine your approach and expand your creative toolkit. Don't be afraid to take risks and push boundaries; it's often in these moments of experimentation that the most distinctive elements of your style will emerge.

Visual storytelling is a cornerstone of directorial style, encompassing everything from camera work and lighting to production design and color palettes. Consider how you frame a scene, the movement of the camera, and the way light interacts with the environment. These choices are not merely technical decisions; they are expressive tools that convey emotion, mood, and meaning. Experiment with different visual techniques to discover which align with your narrative goals and resonate with your artistic sensibilities.

Collaboration with your creative team plays a crucial role in shaping your directorial style. A director is not an isolated artist; they are part of a collective effort to bring a story to life. Working closely with cinematographers, production designers, editors, and actors allows you to refine your vision and explore new possibilities. These collaborations can introduce fresh perspectives and ideas, enriching your work and helping to define your stylistic approach. Building strong relationships with your team fosters a creative environment where experimentation and innovation can thrive.

Storytelling is at the heart of directing, and your style will be deeply connected to how you choose to tell stories. Consider your approach to narrative structure, pacing, and character development. Are you drawn to linear storytelling or do you prefer non-linear narratives that challenge conventional norms? How do you engage with your characters, and what techniques do you use to develop their arcs? These narrative choices are integral to your style, influencing how audiences connect with your work and interpret its meaning.

Emotional resonance is another key element of directorial style, reflecting your ability to evoke emotions and provoke thought in your audience. This involves a delicate balance of narrative, performance, and technical execution, all working in harmony to create a powerful and immersive experience. Consider how you use music, sound design, and silence to heighten emotional impact. Pay attention to the subtleties of performance, guiding actors to deliver nuanced and authentic portrayals. These elements contribute to the emotional depth and empathy that define your style.

The journey to developing a directorial style is ongoing, an evolving process that continues throughout your career. As you grow and change, so too will your style, reflecting new insights, experiences, and influences. Embrace this evolution, allowing your work to be a reflection of your personal growth and artistic exploration. Each project is an opportunity to refine your style, build upon your strengths, and challenge yourself to explore new directions.

In an industry that thrives on both tradition and innovation, finding your unique voice as a director is a powerful asset. It sets you apart, making your work recognizable and memorable to audiences and industry professionals alike. A well-defined style not only enhances your artistic identity but also provides a framework within which you can experiment and innovate.

Communicating with Your Team

Effective communication with your team is the bedrock on which successful film production is built. It's the thread that weaves together the diverse talents and roles within a crew, ensuring that everyone is aligned with the project's vision and objectives. For directors, producers, and other key leaders, mastering the art of communication is essential to fostering a collaborative and efficient working environment where creativity can flourish and challenges are navigated with ease.

At the heart of effective communication is clarity. In the fast-paced and dynamic world of filmmaking, conveying clear and concise instructions is paramount. Ambiguity can lead to misunderstandings, errors, and delays, all of which can derail a production. Whether it's a director explaining the emotional undertones of a scene to actors or a production manager outlining the daily schedule, clarity ensures that everyone understands their role and responsibilities. This clarity is achieved through well-articulated verbal instructions, written documents, and visual aids that leave no room for doubt.

Active listening is an equally important component of communication, creating a two-way street where dialogue and feedback are encouraged. By actively engaging with team members, leaders can gain valuable insights and perspectives that enhance the decision-making process. Listening fosters a sense of respect and inclusion, empowering crew members to contribute their ideas and expertise. This collaborative atmosphere not only boosts morale but also drives innovation as team members feel valued and motivated to go above and beyond in their roles.

Building strong relationships within the team is fundamental to effective communication. A culture of trust and mutual respect paves the way for open and honest dialogue, where team members feel comfortable expressing their thoughts, concerns, and suggestions. This trust is cultivated through consistency, reliability, and a genuine interest in the well-being of each team member. Leaders who demonstrate empathy and understanding create a supportive environment where communication thrives.

Regular meetings and briefings are practical tools for maintaining communication and ensuring that everyone is on the same page. These meetings provide a platform for discussing progress, addressing challenges, and aligning the team with the project's goals. While meetings are essential, they should be purposeful and efficient, respecting the time and contributions of all participants. By setting clear agendas and encouraging focused discussion, leaders can maximize the effectiveness of these sessions and keep the team moving forward.

In the age of digital communication, technology plays a significant role in facilitating interaction among team members. Platforms for messaging, video conferencing, and project management streamline communication, allowing for real-time updates and collaboration. While these tools enhance connectivity, it's important to strike a balance between digital and face-to-face communication. Personal interactions remain invaluable, providing opportunities for nuanced discussions and building stronger interpersonal connections.

Conflict resolution is an inevitable aspect of team communication, as differing opinions and approaches can lead to tension. Addressing conflicts swiftly and constructively is essential to maintaining a harmonious working environment. By approaching conflicts with an open mind and a focus on finding mutually beneficial solutions, leaders can turn challenges into opportunities for growth and learning. This approach not only resolves issues but also strengthens the team's ability to collaborate effectively in the future.

Feedback is a powerful communication tool that drives improvement and development within a team. Constructive feedback helps individuals understand their strengths and areas for growth, while also reinforcing their contributions to the project. Delivering feedback in a respectful and supportive manner encourages a culture of continuous learning and development. Leaders should also be open to receiving feedback from their team, demonstrating a commitment to personal and professional growth.

Celebrating achievements and acknowledging the hard work of the team is an integral part of effective communication. Recognizing milestones, whether big or small, boosts morale and reinforces the collective effort required to bring a project to fruition. Celebrations foster a sense of camaraderie and pride, reminding team members of the impact of their contributions and motivating them to continue striving for excellence.

Cultural sensitivity is another important consideration in team communication, especially in diverse and multicultural environments. Understanding and respecting different communication styles, practices, and values ensures that all team members feel included and respected. By embracing diversity, leaders can harness a wide range of perspectives and ideas, enriching the creative process and enhancing the overall quality of the production.

Balancing Creativity and Practicality

Striking a balance between creativity and practicality is a delicate dance that every filmmaker must master. Filmmaking is an art form that thrives on innovation and originality, yet it is also a process constrained by budgetary, logistical, and temporal realities. Navigating this intersection requires a thoughtful approach that respects both the artistic vision and the practical limitations of production. This chapter delves into the strategies and considerations necessary to achieve this balance, offering insights for both aspiring and seasoned filmmakers.

A clear and compelling vision is the cornerstone of any creative endeavor. It serves as the guiding star that informs every decision, from casting and location scouting to set design and cinematography. However, translating a vision from page to screen is not without its challenges. The first step in balancing creativity and practicality is to distill the essence of the vision, identifying the core elements that are indispensable to the story. By focusing on these key aspects, filmmakers can ensure that the heart of their narrative remains intact, even when adjustments are necessary.

Budget constraints are one of the most significant practical considerations in filmmaking. While it is tempting to dream big, financial resources are often limited. Developing a realistic budget that aligns with the project's creative goals is essential. This involves prioritizing expenditures, identifying areas where costs can be minimized without compromising quality, and being prepared to make tough decisions. For instance, investing in high-quality equipment or experienced talent may yield greater returns than extravagant set pieces or special effects. By understanding where to allocate resources effectively, filmmakers can maintain creative integrity while adhering to budgetary limits.

Logistical planning is another critical aspect of balancing creativity and practicality. Every location, scene, and shot carries logistical implications, from securing permits and coordinating transportation to managing schedules and ensuring safety. A well-organized production plan that accounts for these variables ensures that the creative process runs smoothly and efficiently. This planning requires collaboration between the creative and production teams, fostering an environment where innovative solutions can be found to logistical challenges. Flexibility and adaptability are key, as unforeseen circumstances often arise that require a swift and practical response.

Time management is closely related to both budgetary and logistical considerations. The adage "time is money" holds true in filmmaking, where delays and overruns can lead to increased costs and compromised quality. A detailed shooting schedule that maximizes productivity and minimizes downtime is crucial. This schedule should be realistic, allowing for the unexpected while ensuring that creative goals are met. By adhering to a well-structured timeline, filmmakers can maintain momentum and focus, enabling them to bring their vision to fruition without unnecessary stress or compromise.

Collaboration is at the heart of balancing creativity and practicality. Filmmaking is a collective endeavor, relying on the talents and expertise of a diverse group of individuals. Open communication and mutual respect are essential in fostering a collaborative atmosphere where ideas can be freely exchanged and refined. By valuing the input of all team members, filmmakers can find innovative solutions to practical challenges and enhance the creative process. This collaboration extends beyond the core team to include external partners, such as vendors, locations, and community stakeholders, whose support and cooperation are vital to the project's success.

Technology offers valuable tools for bridging the gap between creativity and practicality. Advances in digital filmmaking, visual effects, and editing software provide filmmakers with new ways to achieve their creative goals within practical constraints. By leveraging technology, filmmakers can experiment with different techniques, streamline workflows, and enhance the overall quality of their work. However, technology should be used judiciously, serving the story rather than overshadowing it. The most effective use of technology complements the creative vision and enhances the narrative.

Risk-taking is an inherent part of the creative process, and balancing creativity and practicality often involves calculated risks. These risks may involve unconventional narrative structures, bold visual choices, or innovative production techniques. While risk-taking can lead to groundbreaking work, it must be tempered with a realistic assessment of potential outcomes and consequences. By carefully weighing the pros and cons, filmmakers can make informed decisions that push creative boundaries while remaining grounded in practical realities.

Compromise is an inevitable part of balancing creativity and practicality, yet it need not be seen as a limitation. Instead, compromise can be a catalyst for creativity, challenging filmmakers to find new ways to achieve their vision within existing constraints. Embracing compromise as an opportunity for growth and innovation empowers filmmakers to think outside the box and discover solutions that might otherwise remain hidden. This mindset fosters resilience and adaptability, qualities that are essential in navigating the ever-changing landscape of filmmaking.

Navigating On-Set Challenges

Every film set is a universe in itself, buzzing with energy and teeming with activity. Within this intricate ecosystem, challenges are as inevitable as the sunrise. Navigating these on-set challenges requires a blend of preparation, adaptability, and resourcefulness, qualities that define an accomplished filmmaker. This chapter delves into the myriad obstacles that can arise during production and offers strategies to manage them effectively, transforming potential setbacks into opportunities for growth and creativity.

At the heart of any successful production lies meticulous planning. Pre-production is where the groundwork is laid, anticipating potential issues and devising strategies to address them before they manifest. A well-thought-out plan includes detailed schedules, contingency plans, and thorough risk assessments, all designed to minimize disruptions and keep the production on track. However, even the best-laid plans can encounter unforeseen hurdles, making flexibility an essential skill for any filmmaker. Embracing the unexpected and adjusting plans on the fly can turn potential pitfalls into creative breakthroughs.

One of the most common challenges on set is managing time effectively. The clock is always ticking, and any delay can have a domino effect, impacting the entire day's schedule and potentially the entire shoot. Ensuring that everyone is aware of call times, prepared for their tasks, and ready to adapt to changes is crucial. This requires clear communication and a well-organized team that understands the importance of punctuality and efficiency. Effective time management also involves recognizing when to push forward and when to allow for creative exploration, striking a balance between maintaining the schedule and fostering innovation.

Technical difficulties are another frequent hurdle, ranging from equipment malfunctions to unpredictable weather conditions. Having a skilled and experienced crew is invaluable in these situations, as their expertise can often resolve issues quickly and efficiently. It's equally important to have backup equipment and contingency plans in place, ensuring that production can continue with minimal interruption. For example, having an alternate indoor location ready when shooting outdoors can save valuable time and resources in case of inclement weather.

Interpersonal dynamics can also present challenges, as film sets bring together a diverse group of individuals, each with their own perspectives, strengths, and working styles. Building a positive, respectful, and collaborative atmosphere is essential for a harmonious set. This begins with clear communication and setting expectations from the outset, emphasizing the importance of teamwork and mutual respect. Encouraging open dialogue and providing opportunities for team members to voice their concerns or suggestions fosters a sense of belonging and investment in the project's success.

Stress and fatigue are inherent aspects of the demanding nature of film production, and addressing them is crucial for maintaining morale and performance. Long hours and intense schedules can take a toll on both the physical and mental well-being of the cast and crew. Implementing measures to support health and well-being, such as regular breaks, nutritious meals, and access to medical care, is essential. Additionally, fostering a supportive environment where individuals feel comfortable discussing their needs and seeking help contributes to a more resilient and productive team.

Creative disagreements are not uncommon on set, as filmmakers and team members bring their individual visions and ideas to the project. While differing opinions can lead to conflict, they can also be a source of innovation and improvement. Navigating these disagreements requires diplomacy and a willingness to listen and compromise. By focusing on the project's goals and encouraging constructive dialogue, filmmakers can harness the diverse perspectives of their team to enhance the final product. Establishing a clear decision-making process, where all voices are heard and considered, helps to resolve conflicts and maintain a cohesive vision.

Safety is a paramount concern on any film set, and addressing safety challenges requires vigilance and proactivity. This involves conducting thorough risk assessments, implementing safety protocols, and ensuring that all team members are trained and informed about potential hazards. Safety meetings and briefings should be a regular part of the production process, reinforcing the importance of safety and providing updates on any changes or concerns. By prioritizing safety, filmmakers protect their team and create an environment where creativity can thrive without compromise.

Despite the best efforts to anticipate and mitigate challenges, unexpected events can still occur. In these moments, adaptability and problem-solving skills are invaluable. Staying calm under pressure and approaching challenges with a positive and proactive attitude can inspire confidence and foster a sense of unity within the team. Encouraging a culture of flexibility and resilience, where challenges are viewed as opportunities for growth, empowers team members to think creatively and collaborate effectively in finding solutions.

Reflecting on challenges and their resolutions is a crucial part of the learning process, providing valuable insights for future projects. By analyzing what worked and what didn't, filmmakers can refine their approaches and enhance their ability to navigate challenges in the future. This reflection also offers an opportunity to celebrate successes and acknowledge the hard work and dedication of the team, reinforcing a sense of accomplishment and pride in their achievements.

Chapter 6

The Art of Cinematography

Understanding Camera Angles and Shots

The art of filmmaking is intrinsically tied to the language of camera angles and shots, each one a brushstroke on the canvas of storytelling. Understanding these elements is crucial for any filmmaker, as they are not merely technical choices but powerful tools that shape the viewer's experience and emotional response. This chapter delves into the nuances of camera angles and shots, offering insights into how they can be employed creatively to enhance narrative depth and visual impact.

Camera angles are the vantage points from which a scene is captured, each offering a distinct perspective that influences the viewer's perception. The high angle, for instance, looks down upon a subject, often diminishing its stature or conveying vulnerability. This angle might be used to depict a character in a moment of weakness or to provide an overview of a scene that highlights the environment over the individual. Conversely, the low angle looks up, imbuing the subject with power and dominance. This perspective can elevate the status of a character, making them appear larger than life, or it can be used to evoke fear and intimidation.

The eye-level angle is the most neutral, placing the viewer on equal footing with the subject. This angle is often employed to create a sense of familiarity and connection, allowing the audience to engage with the character's emotions and experiences without the influence of visual bias. The choice of angle can dramatically alter the storytelling, guiding the audience's emotional journey and emphasizing key themes or character dynamics.

Camera shots, defined by the distance between the camera and the subject, play a pivotal role in framing the narrative. The extreme close-up focuses on minute details, such as a character's eyes or a significant object, drawing attention to subtle nuances and intensifying emotional engagement. This shot is often used to convey intimacy or to highlight crucial narrative elements that might otherwise go unnoticed.

The close-up, slightly wider than the extreme close-up, captures the subject's face or a particular part of the body. It is a powerful tool for eliciting empathy, as it allows the audience to immerse themselves in the character's emotional landscape. By capturing the subtle shifts in expression, the close-up provides insight into the character's inner world, making it a staple in scenes of emotional intensity.

The medium shot, which frames the subject from the waist up, strikes a balance between intimacy and context. It is often used for dialogue scenes, allowing for a clear view of the character's expressions while still providing a sense of their surroundings. This shot facilitates interaction between characters, offering a window into their relationships and dynamics.

The wide shot, or long shot, captures the subject in its entirety, along with a significant portion of the surrounding environment. This shot establishes context, situating the character within their setting and conveying spatial relationships. It is particularly effective in scenes where the environment plays a critical role in the narrative, such as in action sequences or when introducing a new location.

An extreme wide shot, also known as an establishing shot, takes this concept further by capturing a broad view of the environment, often dwarfing the subject within the landscape. This shot is commonly used at the beginning of a scene to set the stage and provide the audience with a sense of place. It can also evoke themes of isolation or grandeur, depending on the context.

The over-the-shoulder shot is a staple in dialogue scenes, framing one character from behind the other, with the focus on the character facing the camera. This shot fosters a sense of intimacy and engagement, placing the audience in the midst of the conversation and allowing them to observe the nuances of interaction from a personal perspective.

The point-of-view shot, or POV, immerses the audience in the character's experience by capturing the scene from their perspective. This shot creates a direct connection between the audience and the character, allowing viewers to see the world through the character's eyes and fostering a deeper emotional engagement.

Dynamic camera movements, such as pans, tilts, and tracking shots, add another layer of complexity to the visual storytelling. A pan involves the horizontal movement of the camera, often used to follow a subject or to reveal new information within the scene. A tilt, on the other hand, involves vertical movement, which can be used to emphasize height or to shift focus from one element to another.

Tracking shots, achieved by moving the camera along a track or with the use of a stabilizer, create a sense of fluid motion and continuity. This technique can be employed to follow a character through a bustling environment, to create tension in a chase sequence, or to provide an uninterrupted view of a scene that unfolds in real-time. The choice of camera movement can significantly enhance the emotional impact and pacing of a scene, guiding the audience's attention and engagement.

The use of camera angles and shots is an art form that requires both technical knowledge and creative intuition. The most effective filmmakers understand how to harness these tools to serve the story, using them to reveal character, convey emotion, and immerse the audience in the narrative world. By experimenting with different angles and shots, filmmakers can discover new ways to express their vision and create a unique cinematic language that resonates with audiences.

Lighting Techniques for Mood and Atmosphere

Lighting is the silent narrator of film, subtly guiding the audience's emotions and perceptions without uttering a single word. It's the tool that can transform a mundane scene into something magical, evoking feelings that resonate deeply with viewers. Understanding how to manipulate light to create mood and atmosphere is a skill that elevates a filmmaker's storytelling capabilities to new heights. This chapter delves into the intricacies of lighting techniques, offering insights on how to harness this powerful element to enhance narrative depth and emotional impact.

The foundation of effective lighting lies in understanding the interplay between light and shadow. This dance determines the visual texture of a scene, influencing how the audience perceives the space and the characters within it. High-key lighting, characterized by bright, even illumination with minimal shadows, often creates a cheerful and open atmosphere. It's commonly used in comedies and musicals, where the mood is light-hearted and the focus is on clarity and vibrancy. The absence of deep shadows in high-key lighting suggests transparency and optimism, inviting the audience into a world that feels safe and inviting.

In contrast, low-key lighting is defined by stark contrasts and deep shadows, creating a sense of mystery, tension, or foreboding. This technique is prevalent in film noir, horror, and thrillers, where the interplay of light and dark mirrors the complexities and uncertainties of the narrative. The shadows in low-key lighting can obscure elements, suggesting hidden truths or lurking dangers, and heighten the emotional stakes by keeping the audience on edge. By selectively illuminating parts of the scene, filmmakers can direct attention and focus, emphasizing key narrative elements while concealing others.

Color temperature is another critical component of lighting design, influencing the emotional tone of a scene. Warm lighting, with its golden hues, evokes feelings of comfort, passion, or nostalgia. It's often used in intimate scenes or to suggest the warmth of a sunset or candlelight. On the other hand, cool lighting, with its bluish tones, can create a sense of detachment, melancholy, or unease. This is particularly effective in scenes set in sterile environments, such as hospitals or laboratories, or in moments of introspection or isolation.

Natural lighting, or the use of available light sources, can lend authenticity and realism to a scene. Shooting during the golden hour—the period shortly after sunrise or before sunset—bathes the scene in soft, diffused light, creating a dreamy and ethereal quality. Conversely, harsh midday sun can be used to convey stark reality or harshness. Understanding how to manipulate natural light, whether by diffusing it with reflectors or enhancing it with additional sources, allows filmmakers to create a desired atmosphere while maintaining a sense of realism.

Artificial lighting offers filmmakers greater control and flexibility, enabling them to craft precise moods and atmospheres. Key lighting, the primary source of illumination, establishes the dominant light direction and intensity in a scene. Fill lighting, positioned opposite the key light, softens shadows and reduces contrast, ensuring that details remain visible without flattening the scene. Backlighting, placed behind the subject, adds depth and separation, creating a halo effect that enhances the subject's presence and adds a sense of mystery or drama.

Practical lighting, where light sources are visible within the frame, can add authenticity and enhance the mood. A flickering candle, a neon sign, or a dimly lit desk lamp can serve as both a narrative element and a source of illumination, blending seamlessly with the scene and contributing to the overall atmosphere. Practical lights can also be used creatively to introduce color and texture, enriching the visual palette and reinforcing the emotional tone.

The use of shadows is a powerful technique for creating mood and atmosphere, capable of conveying depth, tension, or ambiguity. Silhouettes, where the subject is backlit and rendered in shadow, can suggest anonymity or danger, adding intrigue and mystery to a scene. Shadows can also be used to distort or exaggerate features, creating a sense of unease or surrealism. By playing with the size, shape, and movement of shadows, filmmakers can imbue their scenes with a dynamic energy that captivates the audience.

Lighting transitions, such as dimming lights or changing color temperatures, can underscore shifts in mood or narrative. A gradual increase in light can signal hope or revelation, while a sudden plunge into darkness can heighten suspense or signify a turning point. These transitions, when used judiciously, enhance the storytelling by aligning the visual cues with the emotional journey of the characters and the arc of the narrative.

Experimentation is key to mastering the art of lighting. By exploring different techniques and combinations, filmmakers can discover unique ways to express their vision and evoke the desired emotional response. Understanding the principles of lighting is just the beginning; applying them creatively and thoughtfully transforms the technical into the artistic, allowing filmmakers to craft a visual narrative that resonates with audiences on a profound level.

The Role of Color in Film

Color in film is far more than a visual element; it's a potent storytelling device that speaks directly to the emotions, perceptions, and subconscious of the audience. It can subtly influence mood, signify themes, and reveal character traits without a single line of dialogue. Understanding the role of color in film empowers filmmakers to craft a richer narrative tapestry, utilizing this dynamic element to enhance the depth and resonance of their stories.

The psychology of color is a fundamental aspect of its role in film. Each hue carries inherent emotional and cultural associations that can be leveraged to evoke specific responses. Red, for instance, is a color of passion, intensity, and danger. It's often used to heighten tension, signify love, or indicate a warning. Scenes bathed in red light can evoke a visceral, almost primal reaction, drawing the audience into the heightened reality of the moment.

Blue, on the other hand, often signifies calmness, melancholy, or detachment. Its use can evoke feelings of serenity or introspection, as well as coldness or isolation. By washing a scene in blue tones, filmmakers can emphasize themes of longing or introspection, creating a contemplative atmosphere that invites the audience to delve deeper into the emotional undercurrents of the narrative.

Green is associated with nature, renewal, and sometimes envy or corruption. Its dual nature makes it a versatile tool in a filmmaker's palette. A lush, verdant green can symbolize growth and harmony, while a sickly, muted green might suggest decay or moral ambiguity. This color can be used to explore the complexities of human nature, reflecting the duality of innocence and malevolence.

Yellow, a color of warmth and optimism, can also suggest caution or deceit. It embodies the joy of sunlit days as well as the unease of an impending storm. In film, yellow might underscore a character's happiness or naivety, or it could hint at underlying tension or treachery. This multifaceted color allows filmmakers to play with layers of meaning, enriching the visual narrative.

The interplay of colors within a scene conveys deeper layers of meaning. The juxtaposition of contrasting colors, such as red and green, can create visual tension, underscoring conflict or duality. Complementary colors, like blue and orange, can create a harmonious balance that draws the eye and pleases the senses. By carefully selecting and combining colors, filmmakers can craft a visual language that enhances the thematic and emotional depth of their stories.

Color grading in post-production is a crucial step in defining the film's overall aesthetic. This process allows filmmakers to fine-tune the color palette, adjusting hues, contrasts, and saturation to achieve the desired mood and tone. A film might employ a desaturated palette to evoke a sense of nostalgia or realism, or it might use hyper-saturated colors to create a fantastical or heightened reality. Color grading is where the visual identity of the film is solidified, aligning the visual elements with the director's vision.

Historical context and cultural significance also play a role in the use of color in film. Different cultures may ascribe various meanings to colors, influencing how they are perceived by audiences. Filmmakers must be mindful of these nuances, especially in works that aim for authenticity or explore cross-cultural themes. Understanding the cultural connotations of color allows filmmakers to communicate more effectively with diverse audiences, ensuring that their visual storytelling resonates on a global scale.

Symbolism is another powerful aspect of color in film. Colors can serve as visual motifs, reinforcing themes or character arcs throughout a narrative. A character consistently associated with a particular color might embody the qualities or emotions linked to that hue. As the story progresses, changes in the character's color palette can signify transformation or development, providing a visual shorthand for the audience to track their journey.

In addition to its narrative functions, color can also enhance the aesthetic appeal of a film. A well-crafted color palette can elevate the visual experience, drawing audiences into the world of the film and making it more memorable. Filmmakers often draw inspiration from art, nature, and fashion to create striking color schemes that captivate viewers and linger in their minds long after the credits roll.

Experimentation with color allows filmmakers to push the boundaries of traditional storytelling. By challenging conventions and exploring new ways to use color, they can create unique and innovative narratives that surprise and engage audiences. This experimentation might involve unconventional color pairings, unexpected shifts in palette, or the deliberate absence of color to emphasize specific narrative elements.

Working with Cinematography Equipment

Mastering the craft of cinematography begins with understanding and effectively using the equipment that brings a filmmaker's vision to life. From cameras and lenses to lighting gear and stabilizers, each piece of equipment plays a crucial role in capturing the essence of a story. This chapter delves into the essential cinematography equipment, offering insights and practical advice for beginners looking to navigate the complex world of filmmaking tools.

Cameras are the cornerstone of cinematography, with a wide array of options catering to different needs and budgets. Understanding the key features and functionalities of cameras is essential for selecting the right tool for a specific project. Resolution, sensor size, and frame rate are among the critical factors to consider. High-resolution cameras offer greater detail and flexibility in post-production, while larger sensors provide better low-light performance and depth of field control. Frame rate, which determines the number of frames captured per second, influences the motion quality of the footage, with higher frame rates allowing for slow-motion effects.

Beyond technical specifications, ergonomics and usability are important considerations when choosing a camera. A compact and lightweight design is ideal for handheld shooting or when mobility is crucial, while larger cameras might offer more features and connectivity options. It's essential to find a camera that balances technical capabilities with practical usability, ensuring that it complements the filmmaker's style and the demands of the production.

Lenses are the eyes of the camera, shaping the perspective and aesthetic of each shot. The choice of lens can dramatically alter the storytelling, influencing the viewer's perception and emotional engagement. Prime lenses, with fixed focal lengths, offer superior optical quality and larger apertures for low-light situations, while zoom lenses provide flexibility in framing and composition. Understanding the characteristics of different focal lengths is key to choosing the right lens for a specific scene. Wide-angle lenses, for example, emphasize spatial relationships and depth, making them suitable for landscapes or scenes with multiple subjects. Telephoto lenses, on the other hand, compress space and isolate subjects, ideal for portraits or capturing distant action.

Lighting equipment is another fundamental aspect of cinematography, essential for creating mood and atmosphere. From soft, diffused lighting to harsh, directional illumination, the choices made in lighting design can profoundly impact the visual narrative. Continuous lighting, such as LED panels and tungsten lights, offers consistent illumination and allows for real-time adjustments on set. These lights can be modified with diffusers, gels, and reflectors to achieve the desired quality and color temperature. Natural lighting is also a valuable resource, and understanding how to harness and supplement it can elevate the production's visual appeal.

Stabilization equipment ensures smooth and steady shots, crucial for maintaining the audience's immersion in the story. Tripods and monopods provide a stable foundation for static shots, while gimbals and steadicams allow for fluid motion without camera shake. Each type of stabilizer offers unique benefits, and selecting the right one depends on the specific requirements of the scene. For instance, a tripod is ideal for controlled environments where precision is needed, whereas a gimbal excels in dynamic situations requiring mobility and flexibility.

Audio equipment, although often overshadowed by visual elements, is equally important in creating an immersive cinematic experience. High-quality microphones and audio recorders capture the nuances of dialogue and ambient sound, enhancing the storytelling. Shotgun microphones, known for their directional pickup pattern, are ideal for isolating subjects in noisy environments, while lavalier microphones offer discreet placement for capturing dialogue. The choice of audio equipment and its placement can significantly affect the clarity and emotional impact of the sound, making it a critical consideration in cinematography.

Monitoring equipment, such as external monitors and viewfinders, provides filmmakers with accurate representations of their footage, ensuring that the composition, focus, and exposure align with their vision. These tools are invaluable for reviewing shots in real-time, allowing for immediate adjustments and creative decisions. Monitors with advanced features like focus peaking and false color offer additional layers of information, aiding filmmakers in achieving precise and consistent results.

Accessorizing with additional gear can further enhance the cinematographic process. Filters, such as neutral density and polarizers, control exposure and contrast, enabling filmmakers to shoot in challenging lighting conditions and achieve specific visual effects. Follow focus systems offer precise control over lens focus, essential for maintaining sharpness during complex camera movements. Matte boxes and lens hoods reduce lens flare and protect the lens, ensuring optimal image quality.

Safety and maintenance are paramount when working with cinematography equipment. Regular cleaning and inspection prevent technical issues and prolong the lifespan of the gear. Proper storage and transportation minimize the risk of damage, ensuring that the equipment is ready for action when needed. Familiarity with the equipment's operation and troubleshooting procedures is essential for mitigating potential disruptions during production.

The art of cinematography is an ever-evolving field, with technological advancements continually reshaping the landscape. Staying informed about the latest developments and emerging trends empowers filmmakers to make informed decisions and remain competitive in the industry. Workshops, online tutorials, and industry events provide valuable opportunities for learning and networking, fostering growth and innovation.

Capturing Movement and Dynamics

Movement is the heartbeat of cinema, infusing scenes with energy, emotion, and life. Capturing movement effectively is an art that requires both technical skill and creative vision. It involves more than simply following action; it demands an understanding of rhythm, pacing, and the intricate dance between camera and subject. This chapter explores the techniques and considerations involved in capturing movement and dynamics, providing guidance for filmmakers seeking to bring their stories to life through motion.

At the core of capturing movement is the camera itself, the tool that translates physical action into visual language. Camera movement can range from subtle, almost imperceptible shifts to dramatic, sweeping motions that dominate a scene. Each type of movement serves a unique purpose, influencing the viewer's perception and emotional response. Panning, a horizontal movement of the camera, follows a subject across the frame and is often used to reveal new elements, guide the audience's attention, or convey the passage of time. The pace and smoothness of a pan can suggest urgency or tranquility, adding layers of meaning to the narrative.

Tilting, the vertical counterpart to panning, shifts the camera's perspective up or down. This movement can emphasize height, create anticipation, or introduce an element of surprise. A slow tilt upward might reveal a towering structure, evoking awe or intimidation, while a downward tilt could focus on a crucial detail or character, grounding the scene and providing context.

Tracking shots, which involve moving the camera along a path parallel to the subject, create a sense of continuity and engagement. Whether achieved through a dolly, Steadicam, or handheld setup, tracking shots immerse the audience in the action, making them feel as though they are part of the unfolding story. This technique is particularly effective in chase scenes or moments of intense emotion, where the fluidity of movement mirrors the characters' experiences and heightens the audience's connection to the narrative.

The use of cranes or drones elevates the camera, offering a bird's-eye view that can establish setting, suggest omniscience, or convey grandeur. These aerial perspectives provide a unique vantage point that can reveal patterns, relationships, and context that might be lost at ground level. By shifting the viewer's perspective, filmmakers can create a dynamic visual experience that underscores the thematic elements of the story.

In contrast, static shots, where the camera remains fixed, can also convey movement and dynamics through the action within the frame. The choice of a static shot can create tension, focus attention, or highlight the choreography of movement. By allowing the action to unfold organically, filmmakers can emphasize the natural rhythm and flow of the scene, drawing the audience into the moment without distraction.

Slow motion is a powerful tool for capturing movement, allowing the audience to savor and analyze the nuances of action that might otherwise go unnoticed. By extending time, slow motion can heighten drama, emphasize emotion, or reveal subtleties in performance and detail. This technique can transform an ordinary moment into a cinematic spectacle, inviting viewers to engage with the scene on a deeper level.

Conversely, time-lapse photography compresses time, capturing movement that unfolds over hours or days in a matter of seconds. This technique is ideal for illustrating processes, transitions, or the passage of time, offering a unique perspective that can reveal unseen patterns and rhythms. Time-lapse can be used to convey the relentless march of time, the beauty of natural cycles, or the impermanence of man-made structures.

The interaction between camera movement and editing is crucial in shaping the dynamics of a scene. Editing choices dictate the rhythm and pacing, influencing how movement is perceived and experienced. Rapid cuts can create a sense of urgency or chaos, while longer takes allow the audience to absorb the intricacies of motion and performance. The timing of cuts, transitions, and the use of sound can enhance or counterpoint the visual movement, adding complexity and depth to the storytelling.

Lighting also plays a significant role in capturing movement, as it can define the contours, texture, and mood of action. The interplay of light and shadow can accentuate motion, create atmosphere, or focus attention. Dynamic lighting, such as flickering or moving sources, can enhance the perception of movement, while consistent lighting provides clarity and continuity. By carefully considering lighting design, filmmakers can enhance the impact of movement and create a cohesive visual narrative.

Understanding the mechanics of movement is essential, but true mastery comes from experimentation and intuition. By exploring different techniques and styles, filmmakers can develop their own language of motion that reflects their unique vision and storytelling goals. Whether through the fluid grace of a Steadicam shot, the precision of a dolly move, or the visceral energy of handheld footage, capturing movement is a deeply personal and creative endeavor.